Once I started reading this book I couldn't put it down. Linda Jean is an astoundingly honest woman whose story and wisdom will help countless people. Knowing her personally I can say she's someone who doesn't just teach the truth, she lives it. This is a book you'll want to share with everyone you love.
—Gary R. Renard, the best-selling author of *The Disappearance of the Universe* and *Your Immortal Reality*

This is a hell of a book! This autobiography at once embodies the tragedy of human experience and the magnificence of the human spirit.
—Brad Blanton, PhD, the best selling author of *Radical Honesty: How to Transform Your Life by Telling the Truth*

What a story! Yes, one that will resonate with so many people, especially those who've been scarred by past abuse. The central message here is that no matter "what" abuse occurred, there's a liberating formula guaranteed to heal all "effects" both in the perceived past and future . . . a tool that's always available in the ever present now moment; it's called Quantum forgiveness.
—Nouk Sanchez, author of *Take Me to Truth: Undoing the Ego*

For a victim to heal fully there may be no other way to diffuse the anger and resentment one feels than to forgive. Linda is a powerful and exemplary example of this truth. A must read for all who are seeking to heal.
—Azim Khamisa, author of *Azim's Bardo: From Murder to Forgiveness*

Linda speaks for a generation of "free spirits" who buried their pain in the fast lane, with a constant turnover in lovers, jobs, and cities. But the pace of her story really picks up when she heals her wounds and discovers her true nature. Only then does she truly become a free spirit. This book of her courageous journey, a real page-turning adventure, will inspire countless others to let go of their past pains and addictions to become truly free. The trip to Hawaii reminded me of Shirley MacLaine in Out on a Limb.
—Susan Schenck, author of *The Live Food Factor: A Comprehensive Guide to the Ultimate Diet for Body, Mind, Spirit & Planet*

Written with such honesty from the heart, the love and care throughout the book is inspiring. Linda writes from her own life and how she turned her pain around with the message of True Forgiveness. I applaud Linda for her courage to share herself with such authenticity. This book will undoubtedly make a tremendous difference to many people.
—Karen L. Renard

This is a powerful story for anyone who is looking for true change. It will help you break the cycle of pain and suffering that we unwittingly and unconsciously create. It illuminates a path to climb out of our own self-created hell. Forgiveness will lead you to your light and give your life back to you. I know because I have been to hell.
—Inmate# 035687-061, Lexington Federal Prison

I sat down to read the first section of One Again—*and I was hooked! I read it straight through, cover-to-cover, and I am so glad I did—it's a marvelous journey filled with memorable real-life characters and personal courage. Give this book to someone on a similar path who can use a real boost from one who has been there and offers hope and substance on the journey.*
—Diane Campbell, MD

From the first pages, Linda's story grabbed me by the throat! Her attention to the detail, and the musical flow of things encouraged me to find myself in this novel. As a patient guide, Linda is able to help anyone find peace and forgiveness, in the turmoil of everyday life. This masterpiece of human emotion works up to a spiritual platform that will allow you to find your true self.
—Johan Oeyen, trustee of the Tariq Khamisa Foundation; Stopping Kids from Killing Kids (TKF), San Diego, CA

I love it and could hardly put it down! Your realness, humanness, humor, and forgiveness; depth of your journey and love of God inspires me to my core and has left me deeply touched. I honor and give you my sincere love and blessings; for you have walked the road less traveled. This human family is so blessed to have you serving us.
—Brian Matthew Self, CNH, MH, CCI, natural health and lifestyle coach

Nothing is as fast moving as an idea whose time has come. This is our way out of the Hell we have created on this planet. All the saints have told us forgiveness is love and if we love, we forgive! I feel in my bones that this book is going to bring transformation to many in our society.
—Pamela Nees, program director of Optimum
Health Institute, Lemon Grove, CA

Linda, I want you to know that I have been reading your book during my lunch hours and have at times been unable to stop reading . . . What a life you've had, it was like a roller coaster ride for self-discovery. I have read it all and I loved it. I would totally recommend it to my friends, and already have.
—Tracy Firmino, banker

I recommend all to read this book, as it will help to forgive the past, while remaining in the present, giving hope for a better future. This book is a guide for those who have suffered in the past at the hands of others.
—Hira Ratan Manek, teacher of Solar Healing

This is truly an inspiring story that allows its readers to follow the life of a woman, as she is brought out of Hell into a life of beauty and freedom. It offers everyone an opportunity to see the power of true forgiveness at work, which if applied to anyone's life, has the power to completely alter the course of that life.
—Samuel Riche

ONE
AGAIN

ONE
AGAIN

A TRUE STORY OF A DIFFERENT KIND OF FORGIVENESS

LINDA JEAN McNABB

HAMPTON ROADS
PUBLISHING COMPANY, INC.

Cover design by Frame25 Productions
Cover art by konstantynov c/o Shutterstock.com, Galyna Andrushko c/o Shutterstock.com,
juliengrondin c/o Shutterstock.com, Hermínia Lúcia Lopes Serra c/o Shutterstock.com,
ukrphoto c/o Shutterstock.com

Hampton Roads Publishing Company, Inc.
1125 Stoney Ridge Road
Charlottesville, VA 22902

434-296-2772 • fax: 434-296-5096
e-mail: hrpc@hrpub.com
www.hrpub.com

If you are unable to order this book from your local
bookseller, you may order directly from the publisher.
Call 1-800-766-8009, toll-free.

Library of Congress Cataloging-in-Publication Data

McNabb, Linda Jean.
    One again : a true story of the power of a different kind of forgiveness /
Linda Jean McNabb.
        p. cm.
    Summary: "A personal memoir of the author's tragic life and how she
overcame many physical and emotional obstacles to become 'one again' with
God"--Provided by publisher.
    ISBN 978-1-57174-610-8 (tp : alk. paper)
    1. McNabb, Linda Jean. 2. Spiritual biography. 3. Spirituality. 4.
Forgiveness--Religious aspects. 5. Spiritual life. I. Title.
    BL73.M388A3 2009
    204.092--dc22
    [B]
                                    2009002474

ISBN 978-1-57174-610-8
10 9 8 7 6 5 4 3 2 1
Printed on acid-free paper in the United States

This book is dedicated to Beej, Mom,
Michael, Cathy, and Tommy—
my greatest spiritual teachers.

A NOTE FROM THE AUTHOR

The process of writing this book reminded me of what it was like to work as a professional organizer. When I used to organize a space for a client, the first step was to tear everything apart, revealing all the clutter and debris. I then discarded the trash and organized what remained—the beautiful and the useful—being careful to leave no stone unturned.

In much the same way, I have allowed that which no longer serves me to surface from my unconscious and become undone, leaving me with only what is beautiful and useful. It is through this metamorphosis that I am able to actually practice my true calling. I had to clear away the clutter of the ego mind in order to see the horizon of a new dawn, and I hope that those reading this book will be inspired to do the same. I must warn you, though—your circumstances might appear to get worse before they get better, which is sometimes part of the process. Don't believe in appearances and remain true to what your heart is telling you. That will be enough to carry you through to the other side, where you will never want for anything ever again. That we appear to be here on this Earth is proof enough of our insanity. And our insanity is nothing more than imagining that we are separate from God.

I now see that the greatest love story is the one we have with God. Nothing in this world can take the place of that. All else surely pales in comparison. Until I return home, I'll do my level best to use what I have to communicate that truth and make the best of a difficult situation. Nonetheless, I wouldn't say to someone, "Hey baby, I'm sorry; but God is the one I'm really hot for, not you." In the past I was interested in what other people could do and be for me while trying to be what they needed me to be. Now I hope that I'm able to love, give to, and care for another as God would, not needing anything in return. I hope that I will do this, not only with a romantic partner, my family, and close friends, but with everyone, everywhere as we each make our way Home.

Where I once built my house on the sand bluffs of an illusion that easily crumbles and falls away, I now build my house on a foundation of solid rock, which is God. *A life well forgiven is a life worth living.*

—Linda Jean McNabb

— PART ONE —

She feels empty,
Although no one knows,
She is reaching out
For what, she may never know.
She chooses to sit in silence,
And hope that someone stumbles across
Her and all of her loneliness.

She only hopes that they will find her in time
Before she drifts too far away,
As she slowly lets go,
Of whatever grasp she has left of the world
As she slowly fades away,
Nearly unnoticed . . . .

—Sarah M. Montesi

INTRODUCTION

On August 6, 1957, I was born, insane. Things pretty much went downhill from there.

Forty-eight years later, on Easter Day 2006, I found myself on the North Shore of the island of Kauai in Hawaii, homeless and broke. I had been through a lot: rape, self-loathing, alcoholism, wild spending sprees, bankruptcies, more than fifty moves, and almost as many Mr. Wrongs. Not to mention an addiction to junk food, a three-pack-a-day cigarette habit, the untimely deaths of several family members, countless soul-deadening menial jobs, a short stint into prostitution, and a lifelong, nearly overpowering depression that had led me to consider suicide many times in my life. And now here I was: alone, no money, no idea what to do next. I could have admitted defeat, flown back to the mainland with the last of my money, and tried to pick up the pieces of my life one more time, but an insistent voice inside me kept saying one thing: I should hike into Na Pali Coast—one of the toughest hikes in the world.

I called my friend Wei, a Chinese man I'd met meditating on the beach who had become a spiritual mentor, and told him that for some inexplicable reason I felt compelled to go into the woods. Getting right within myself and finding a way to be at peace was my driving force. Nothing else mattered. Wei met me at the North Shore the day before I planned to hike in. He offered me some packaged food, but I declined. I was taking fruit and understood there was plenty more growing wild in the valley. If not, I figured I'd fast and drink water. I told him that I *had* to go, even though the trail was closed and the river was high. Wei said, "No problem. Problem is only in the mind. Do not worry." I laughed and said, "Okay." Despite my determination, I was frightened. I had no idea what the hell I was doing. I was blindly following my heart, not knowing what to expect on the trail ahead.

The next day I finished packing and got a ride from my friend Bert up to the North Shore. Bert became quite impatient with me when he saw my huge overstuffed backpack. He said, "Can you even pick that up? This is a serious trail. Do you have any idea what you're doing? You need to be able to stand on one leg with your pack on." I could barely stand on two legs while holding the pack, so I didn't try with just one. I knew Bert thought I was crazy. I silently concurred.

After Bert dropped me off, I hitchhiked. A man in a truck soon picked me up. He had to help me lift the backpack into the back of his pickup. A big bottle of water slipped out of a pocket of my pack into the bed of the truck; I wouldn't notice that it was missing until I was on the trail. It was the only water I was carrying; I planned to drink from the river once inside. I'd tried to borrow a portable water filter, but it hadn't worked out and there had been no time to buy one. Besides, my limited money supply was dwindling. The man in the truck dropped me off about a mile from the entrance to the trail and drove off with a friendly wave.

By the time I reached the entrance to the trail, I was already tired. My pack was so heavy it was a struggle to walk. The temperature was warm and gentle rain fell off and on. I was scared out of my wits, but it didn't matter. Something inside me pushed me forward.

Here I was, about to hike a trail that was dangerous under the best of conditions. People had lost their lives on this trail. I was toting a backpack that I could barely carry, and the trail was officially closed due to the past forty days of heavy rains. I had never hiked anything like this, or even camped out before. Other than that, it was a perfect plan. *Problems are only in the mind.* I was going in to fix what was broken. I was going in to learn how to live, even if it killed me.

CHAPTER ONE

The name of the trail I felt compelled to hike is Kalalau Trail. My plan was to hike ten miles into the Kalalau Valley and set up camp for an extended stay. A healthy, experienced hiker properly outfitted could hike this trail in eight hours or less. It took me two-and-a-half days to cover the ten miles to the bluffs. My giant backpack was symbolic of how I'd felt all my life; I was carrying the weight of the world on my shoulders.

I set off at midday and began walking as best as I could. I had to; I was following some internal boss whose voice was inaudible to others yet so loud on a spiritual level that it was impossible for me to ignore. I felt like a robot carrying out orders. For the first two miles I frequently crossed paths with other hikers. Every time we passed each other, they'd all look at me and someone would say, "That sure looks like a heavy pack." Each time I smiled and nodded cheerily, like I always did, pretending everything was fine. People could now see what a heavy load I carried, in my mind and on the trail, because I was literally hauling it on my back.

I carried a walking stick to help me with my balance. With such a big pack, it was impossible for me to be completely balanced, but the stick helped. Every so often I sat on a big rock, leaned my pack against it, and rested my legs. After hiking for only a couple of hours, I realized my water bottle was missing. I could see it in my mind, bouncing around the back of the kind stranger's pickup. I ate some little tangerines instead. It rained off and on, all day and all night. The trail became increasingly difficult, and I knew I was really in for it.

The first day I hiked for about six hours, until it started to get dark. I was worn out and in pain. I pulled out a tarp and spread it on the ground, pulling it over my pack and me so we'd be protected from the rain. The ground was slanted and I kept sliding downhill all night, so I got very little sleep. At least there were no animals or snakes to fear; there were no predators on the entire island. At some point during that long night I heard my deceased brother Michael's voice, telling me that he had the perfect camping spot picked out for me and that someone would show me the way. In the morning, I ate more tangerines and set my pack on a big rock, making it as easy as possible to slip on. My muscles, especially in my neck and my thighs, screamed in protest when the pack came back on.

All day it continued to rain off and on. I reached the five-mile marker, where I had to cross the river. It wasn't too wide, but it was high, and the force of the water rushing downhill toward the ocean was extremely powerful. It could easily have carried me to my death. Normally, a permit would be required to hike farther or to camp overnight, but due to the conditions no permits were being issued at all. A sign warned that the river was extremely dangerous and to cross it meant risking death. The warnings were sobering, and I had to summon all my courage to enter the river. The thought of turning back still didn't cross my mind. When I stepped into the rushing current, the water was above my waist. I immediately slipped and fell over sideways.

Even with the weight of my backpack and the strong current dragging me down, I stayed calm and still. I wedged my feet into the bottom of the river between slippery rocks while crouching underwater, then managed to right myself and regain my bearings. One step at a time, I found a foothold and made my way across the loud, rushing water, using my walking stick and every ounce of energy to keep myself from being pulled downriver by the strong current. Finally, I made it across. I sprawled out on the ground, supremely, royally, largely, hugely, thank-you-God-for-saving-a-wretch-like-me relieved.

Shortly after leaving the river, I lost the trail as I descended through the woods. When I realized I was off the trail, I retraced my path and eventually picked it up again. That little detour took three hours or more. I had started the day tired; that mistake used up most of what little energy I had left. After the five-mile marker, other hikers were few and far between. I was literally hiking up and down mountains. Sometimes the trail was steep, other times it flattened out. Sometimes it was on the outside of a mountain, sometimes it was through dense woods.

When I was on the outside of a mountain, the narrow trails were so slippery with overgrown brush that it was difficult to keep from sliding off. The danger, apart from falling all the way down to the ocean or the valley floor to my immediate death, was that I might get hung up somewhere in between and lie helpless and injured. If that happened, I might not be found in time to be rescued. I was hiking on mountains thousands of feet above the ocean, where at any minute I could easily plummet to my death. The closer I came to the edge of death, the closer I was to life, a new life.

Each time I scaled a higher mountain, I thought the worst was over and that it would get easier. But it didn't. The trail kept getting harder and more dangerous. All day long helicopters buzzed overhead. I was afraid of being seen, but most of the time there was nothing I could do because I was out in the open. I'd later learn that they were tours, rangers, or the Drug Enforcement Agency looking for marijuana.

By late afternoon of the second day, I arrived at possibly the most harrowing part of the trail. I looked out and down the mountain, where an extremely narrow and steep path traversed it. It was hard to imagine how anyone could hike it without sliding down the face of mountain. I said out loud, "You'd have to be a billy goat to hike that." Still, I began to descend the trail very carefully, one step at a time, which is the only way I'd made it as far as I had. Instead of thinking ahead, or about how far I had to go, or about how much I was hurting, I looked at my feet and willed them to move, one foot in front of the other, one step, then another, then another. It wasn't easy because of the weight and balance of my backpack. The entire trail was still wet and slippery from the rain. Each step had to be carefully placed, measured, and slowly executed. At each step I risked losing my footing.

As I was slowly making my way, a barefoot man with long hair, a beard, and no pack easily whizzed past me, down the side of the mountain and up the next. He must have been one of the local residents of the forest that I'd heard stories about. He was out of sight in a minute, nimble as a real billy goat.

I cautiously continued down the mountain and ascended the next . . . until I found myself on a narrow slippery path barely one foot-width wide. It was windy, so I faced the mountain walking sideways, leaning into and hugging the mountain so that I wouldn't lose my balance and be blown off the path. Behind me there was only air—and an unobstructed view to the rocky shores of the ocean below. As I hiked around the mountain, I was faced with a straight ascent up the mountain. It looked impossible, but I did it. Then, as I sat at the top and rested, I looked around and realized that I couldn't find the trail.

I looked over the edge of the mountain and saw what might have been the remnants of a trail washed away by the rain. I looked behind me and there was a ribbon of rock that went straight up. I couldn't see past it. Looking around from where I was sitting, it appeared that the trail must have been washed away. I looked at the trail I'd just descended. I sat there and pondered my situation for a time, thinking there had to be a way and having a hard time accepting that there wasn't. I didn't want to go back the difficult and dangerous way I'd just come, but decided I had no choice.

Out there on those treacherous mountain trails a person gets in touch with his or her will to live very quickly. On the face of that mountain, with a few small inches between death and me, it became clear that death was not what I desired. I felt my mom and sister Cathy calling out to me. For the first time in my life I realized how much I wanted to live. I yelled out, "Okay, you win, I do not want to die." As I crawled back along the mountain ledge, shivering from the biting wind, hugging the mountain, and feeling warmed by the heat and smell of the sun-soaked stone, I vowed, "I do not care what I have to do. I will find a place and set up my tent. I will rest a while and then hike back out. I will go back into town and work any job and do anything to survive. I give up. I give up. I give up." I made my way back through the billy goat trail all the way up to a safer place to rest.

From out of nowhere, a man appeared and I found myself looking up into his face. He was shirtless and carried a large duffle bag by sticking his head through the handles so the bag hung down his back. He walked with a stick and was older with gray hair and a gray beard. He said to me in a thick European accent, "How are you doing?" I said, "Not very good. I was on my way into the forest to camp, but I lost the trail and I'm giving up." He said, "Don't be ashamed. I have seen grown men turn back from this part of the trail. Would you like me to carry your pack for you?" I looked at him, barely believing this miracle. "Thank you, yes," I said.

He set his bag down and took mine. He was off, descending down the billy goat trail and up the other mountain. He moved so quickly that I lost sight of him. I followed after him, still in pain, but the trip was much lighter and easier without the pack. I soon made my way back to where I'd recently lost sight of the trail and turned back. He'd already passed me on his way back to retrieve his own bag, and pointed to where the trail was. I climbed up and over the narrow ribbon of rock I'd recently been stuck on. There, down below, was the trail—it was only a couple of feet away from where I'd been sitting. My pack was down there waiting; I walked over and maneuvered it back on. It was difficult. By now, it was nearing the end of the day. I was exhausted, sore, and worn to a frazzle.

When the man caught up to me again, he told me his name was Hamlet and that we were nearing the helicopter landing at the eight-mile mark, about a half-mile from where we had met. He suggested we camp there for the night. We hiked on. At another difficult point of the trail, he simply set his bag down and took my pack again. I followed him until he set my pack down. Once again he hiked back to retrieve his own bag. I sat down. I did not think I'd be able to carry my pack any farther. When Hamlet caught back up with me, I asked him for help. He set his bag down and picked mine up, though he admonished that I shouldn't become dependent upon him.

We finally made it to the campsite. I told Hamlet that I hadn't drunk any water for two days, and he steered me to the nearby river. When I returned, we used my two tarps as a floor and a roof. Hamlet expertly constructed a shelter for us by fastening one of the tarps between some trees with bungee cords. Hamlet offered me a powdered drink mix that I declined, because I thought it had too much sugar in it. I shared the last of my tangerines with him. I told him how grateful I was for his help and assured him that the next day I'd be fine to go on my own. Normally Hamlet would have made it into the valley to his camp. Because he stopped to help me, he ran out of daylight. We slept, but I kept waking up from the sound of the tarp being whipped by the wind.

The next morning, we were up bright and early—or did we even sleep? Hamlet told me that there were a few more sections of the trail ahead that were dangerous and that he'd carry my pack through them for me. I thanked him, telling him he'd already done enough. He stuck by me though. He asked me many questions: Was I a writer? "Yes," I said. "How'd you know?" He asked about my spiritual beliefs. After I shared some of them, he asked if I'd ever studied Buddhism or Eastern philosophies. I told him I hadn't but that lately I'd skimmed through some of those teachings and felt some of them resonate within me.

As we hiked the rest of the trail, Hamlet told me that he knew of a perfect spot for me. I suddenly remembered my brother's words from my first night on the trail. Hamlet ushered me along. It wasn't easy; by now, my feet had open blisters where the straps of my sandals rubbed, which made hiking difficult, but I knew the end of the difficulties was near. I'd soon be able to crawl inside my tent and pass out for as long as I needed. Hamlet carried my pack over the more difficult passes. There were some places where the mountainside looked like a mountain of red dirt with no discernible path. It appeared that you'd have no choice but to simply slide down the mountain into the ocean below. But somehow, I was able to remain upright and on-track. Although in one place I wanted to squat and crawl, Hamlet was able to talk me through it. When we came to more heavy brush, Hamlet cut through it with a small machete he carried with him, making it much easier to pass through. He told me that we'd reach the bluffs by noon.

Finally, we had one last huge slick red mountain to pass. Hamlet instructed me to lean into his back and he'd guide me across this last pass. It was a difficult descent, especially with my feet torn up. We finally made it to the woods. Hamlet led me back to a place under the cover of the forest, near a clearing on the bluffs. Huge rocks had been arranged to form camps and gardens many years ago by the original settlers of the island.

It started to rain again as Hamlet quickly set up my tent between four trees. He fastened a tarp to the trees over the top of the tent for protection from the rain. He told me that he'd come back for a visit in a week or so and would show me around Kalalau Valley. Hamlet hiked in and out of Kalalau twice a month to pick up his mail, food, and supplies. He had a feral cat buddy he called Cat waiting for him back at his camp. Then he was gone as suddenly as he had appeared.

I removed my hiking sandals and set them outside of my tent. My whole body relaxed into joy to finally be free of the torturous hiking sandals and heavy pack. Fortunately, I had my comfortable old flip-flops to wear. I unpacked and organized my stuff. What a tremendous relief it was to be there at last. I doubt that I'd ever felt such gratitude in my entire life. Just to have survived the trail, to still be alive and in one piece, was quite something to me. The trail was a transforming experience in and of itself. Now came life!

— CHAPTER TWO —

Despite my elation, I was covered with dirt. My fingernails and toenails were packed with mud, and my clothes were filthy. I cleaned myself up the best I could and hiked to fill my plastic collapsible water jug, finding some guava fruit along the way. I ran into a man named Nathaniel, one of a handful of "outlaws" who lived in the forest and valley. Years ago they had been legal residents, but no longer, hence their nickname. He invited me to join him and some other campers for pizza that evening. I declined the invitation because I only ate all raw food. Not to mention the fact that all I wanted to do was lie down and do nothing but sleep for a few days. I could barely walk and leaned heavily on my walking stick to alleviate some of the pain.

I concluded that no one person actually owns or governs any land or place in the entire universe. Ownership is just an illusion. I felt that I had every right to be in the Kalalau Valley for as long as I chose. I stayed for eighteen days, and the rangers did not find me. Four others, whom I met near my camp, were found and cited. I encountered a few of the other outlaws, and they were all very helpful, kind, and generous. There were only a handful of them, living there taking care of the land, cultivating gardens, and speaking to the visitors about packing out what they packed in. I learned that they often collected trash that campers had left behind and placed it down on the beach, where the rangers could easily collect it.

Wei had warned me that I'd go through a high level of detoxification and purification on my journey. He'd given me a tiny statue of Buddha and a bracelet made of Buddha Beads along with a chant to say while rubbing the beads between my fingers if the pain became too intense. As I lay down to sleep the first night in camp, I realized my tent was pitched on top of thick tree roots and on a slight slant, once again causing me to slide as I slept. It was difficult, if not impossible, to get comfortable, but I slept the best I could. By the next morning, my thighs were so sore I could barely crouch to urinate.

I ate guava fruit for the first three days in camp—until my stomach turned and I had to stop. I discovered that there was plenty of fruit in the forest, but most of it would not be ripe for at least a couple more months. I mostly just drank water. There was a garden nearby that was cared for by the outlaws and regular visitors. Every day or so, there would be a few ripened papayas, so that is what I had to eat. After two or three days, I stopped having bowel movements—that was a first. I felt very light and weak.

The blisters on my feet became infected, so it was still painful to walk. I didn't feel well enough to make it to the river to bathe until about the third or fourth day. As my muscle aches began to subside, I developed intense sinus headaches that were especially painful when I lay down to sleep at night. I couldn't recall ever experiencing sinus pain that severe; I used the beads and chant that Wei had given me. From the first night, I had vivid dreams, visions, insights, and knowing. I was "told" that a wealthy and famous actress would be so moved by my book that she'd be instrumental in having it made into a movie.

After four nights, the headaches subsided and finally faded away until not even a hint of pain was left. Hamlet brought me a

couple of oranges one morning. My feet were still sore, but over-
all I was feeling better. One of my toenails became infected and
eventually fell off. Hamlet told me that my own saliva would heal
the infections, which proved to be true. I followed Hamlet down
to the beach. As we passed through various gardens along the way,
he picked herbs and greens to eat later. I hurriedly limped along,
never quite able to keep up with him. There were remnants of a
community library and outdoor kitchen along one wall of a natural cove, very near to the beachfront campsites below a waterfall
thirty feet high.

Hamlet told me how he'd lived in the woods for the past few
years. He said he was originally from Europe and had spent time
in a concentration camp with his sister when they were small children, guarded by horribly cruel and inhumane guards. The stories
were heartbreaking. I shared with Hamlet the story I was planning
to write and what had brought me to the forest. We spent most of
the day hiking and foraging for food companionably. Hamlet was
a gentle man, who had lived alone for years but was a friend to
many.

At the end of the day I told him that I did not want to hike
back out—I'd heard from the outlaws that boats sometimes carried people out of the valley. He told me of a native Hawaiian man
who owned a boat and provided such a service. He handed me a
hundred-dollar bill, saying, "I have plenty of money. This will get
you back to town." I gratefully accepted his offering and thanked
him for his generosity. As late afternoon settled in around us, we
hiked back toward the bluffs and then said our good-byes. I'd be
gone before he'd be back that way again.

I spent the next two weeks quietly resting, showering in the
waterfall by the beach or bathing in the river, never quite becoming accustomed to the chill of the water. Every couple of days, I
rinsed and freshened my clothes in the river, hanging them to dry

at my camp. I started out with a few papayas, a few oranges, some nuts, and water. Many days I had only water. I hiked around and did some exploring, sometimes on my own or occasionally with other campers. I showed them a small group of orange trees that Hamlet had told me about. Most of the oranges were still green and a month away from being ripe enough to eat. Each trip to the orange trees included at least several failed attempts to obtain the one or two oranges that were ripe enough to eat. If we were lucky, we were able to shake a couple loose, which were divided up and devoured on the spot.

Because I was eating so little, I got tired very easily and had to pace myself. I enjoyed hiking down to the beach to walk barefoot on the sand, but I had to go especially early or the sand was like hot coals. I did make it into the valley a couple of times and to some huge caves on the beach. I sunbathed in the nude and walked on the beach *au naturel.* It was a liberating experience, and one that I'd never before experienced.

The other campers had nightly parties to which I was invited. I declined, preferring to be inside my tent by sundown when the mosquitoes were at their worst. It was cold at night, even with two sleeping bags, long pants, and two shirts. Much of what I'd brought was unnecessary, and I gave away what I could. I met a young man who had hiked from Mexico to Canada, twice, and to many other places. I inquired as to what he carried in his backpack. He knew the exact weight of everything in his pack to the ounce and had it down to a science. I learned a great deal from him. He came over to my tent to see what I'd packed. After laughing at my gigantic floss, he pointed out that my huge torch lighter could have been replaced with a tiny one. I told him the worst part was that since I wasn't cooking I had no use for it. I'd thought I might need it so I just packed it. There were many other items like that, along with clothes I didn't need either.

I could view the sunset each night by looking out the front of my tent and peeking through the trees. When I hiked to the beach, the view of the coastal mountains was beyond magnificent. There was one place where they resembled a heavenly cathedral. The entire coast held some of the most indescribably beautiful fantastic sights I'd ever seen in my life.

After camping for two-and-a-half weeks with very little to eat, I was feeling pretty weak. Something told me it was time to go. I made arrangements to be picked up at the beach the next afternoon by Jet Ski. The charge was two hundred dollars, reduced to one hundred dollars for me, since that was all I had. I gave my tent and camping supplies to one of the men who was on an extended stay; my hiking sandals were a perfect fit for a young woman who'd recently lost a shoe in the river. The man to whom I gave my tent carried the rest of my belongings down to the beach for me. I showered in the beachfront waterfall and made myself comfortable under the shade of a tree on the sand. I fell asleep. The sand made a comfortable bed, and that nap turned out to be the best sleep of my stay.

Day turned into night, and no Jet Ski. The man I hired had been so adamant about his dependability that I waited until it was too dark for me to hike back up to the bluffs. Some campers shared some cooked food with me, my first in over two years. Later, the unfamiliar food tore up my stomach and digestive tract, causing me to become violently sick with cramps.

I was now miserably ill and had no tent when it started raining. A young woman in the group chewed me out for being so irresponsible. She hoped that I would not do this to myself again. She was young enough to be my daughter. I didn't debate the matter with her. I climbed on top of a huge covered wooden storage locker under a roof with my sleeping bag and slept the best I could despite agonizing cramps. At least I was dry.

The next morning, I woke up early and went back to the beach under the tree. I waited again for the Jet Ski, but he didn't show up the second day either. This time, an older woman at a nearby campsite who had heard my story was keeping an eye out for me. When my ride out had not yet arrived an hour before sunset, she offered me shelter at her campsite. She generously shared some food and made a "tent" for me out of a spare tarp. Early the next morning, she packed up and bid me farewell as I thanked her for her help and kindness. During the previous two nights mosquitoes had ravaged my face, covering it with itchy red bites.

I decided that I did not care if the Jet Ski ever arrived. There was nowhere I had to be. So I retrieved an abandoned tent and a clean sleeping bag that someone had left behind. If I was going to stay, at least I would be safe from the mosquitoes. Just as I finished pitching the tent, two women approached. They'd hiked in with their husbands the night before, and one of the husbands was pretty beat up. The other husband had left early that morning to send for a boat. The women were frightened because the trail was so dangerous. They'd heard about me through the grapevine, and asked if I'd like to leave with them on the boat.

I thanked them for thinking of me. I explained that the currents were very strong and that I was not a good swimmer, so I would not be able to swim to the boat. The women said that the boat would come right up on the sand. Just then, they saw another boat dropping off two women. They raced out to where the boat was. I went about my business, getting some water for the day and using the bathroom. They called out to me as I was on my way back from the waterfall. They'd hired the boat to take them back and there was plenty of room for me. But we all had to swim to the boat. Boogie boards would be provided, and we'd be coached on how to get there. They pointed to where the boat was and told me to bring my things out to the beach if I wanted to go back with them.

I packed up my belongings. They were pretty well water-proofed in a big black garbage bag I'd prepared for the ride on the Jet Ski. I dragged my bag out to the beach and watched the others swim to the boat. Once they were past the break point, they were home free; it was just getting past it that was tricky. It would throw you right back if you didn't swim hard enough. There were five people including myself being picked up. Two of the people made it to the boat. The wife of the man who was hiking out alone was very worried about her husband and couldn't get past the breakers. She kept getting tossed back.

I gave myself a little pep talk. I asked my guardian angel or whoever might be listening to step forward and help me, because I was going in. I'd been scared of deep water ever since my brother Tommy had drowned when we were children; I had rarely gone into the water in all the years since. One of the things that most frightened me was the idea of cold water. I suddenly remembered how I'd cried all those years ago, thinking that Tommy must have been so cold. I was surprised that this water was so warm.

I picked up a boogie board and walked over to the young man who was doing the coaching. I told him, "Tell me what to do and I'll do it." He swam with me out toward the breakers and told me to kick like hell. I did, and I made it past. I was on board before I knew it. I was no longer afraid of the water. Now, all I had to do was conquer my fear of being eaten by "Jaws." The wife who was having trouble finally made it to the boat, completely worn out.

The ride back to Hanalei seemed like a long one. It was a much different perspective viewing the mountains from the water, whizzing by the trail that had taken me days to cross. I was so grateful to not be hiking back, especially since my feet were not completely healed and I was still limping. I knew that my paradise was not in the forest; it was within me. I also knew that whatever I was looking for was inside me too. I knew that no matter how much our loved ones care about us and want us to stay alive, we are the only ones who can make the choice to live. I emerged from my adventure with a much greater will to live than when I went in.

CHAPTER THREE

When I was growing up, our dad loved telling us kids about the time he borrowed his future father-in-law's car and eloped with our mom when they were teenagers. Telling this story made Dad happy; he smiled, laughed, and held us on his lap. He'd always hold up an old photograph to illustrate the story, and we four kids gazed rapt at the two of them—so beautiful, so filled with hope, and so very, very young.

This was one of the good times. Other times, the abuse was like a haunting ghost that might show up anytime, maybe for a minute, maybe longer. It was not a question of if; it was a question of when. As in *A Tale of Two Cities,* "It was the best of times. It was the worst of times." To the outside world, we appeared to be a typical suburban middle-class family, living the American dream:

Drive-in movies. *Planet of the Apes.* Country Squire station wagon with fake wood paneling. Lying in the back on cool summer nights, dark skies, bright stars, his giant feet up on the back window leaving big footprints next to our tiny ones. Body heat generating condensation on the glass. Snack bar. Ice cream bars. Licking. Munching. Dad smiling ear to ear as he lay in between us, just a big kid, all of us wiggling and giggling around him under the twinkling night sky in a sea of cars at the drive-in.

Summer vacation. Mom, Dad, kids, loaded-up station wagon, suitcases, food hamper, off down the highway traveling to many faraway destinations. Wide-eyed, happy as baby birds gawking at the White House, Washington Monument, Lincoln Memorial, Smithsonian Institute. Authentic arrowhead at Gettysburg. Homes of Jefferson, Lincoln, Thomas Edison. Riding to the top of the St. Louis Arch, Dad so totally and utterly fascinated by its architecture and construction. Happy times.

Sad times. Lying face down on carpeted floor in front of the big black-and-white television, loud bawling, crying, face soaked, snot running. Shirley Temple movie not showing this week. Snowstorm outside. God punishing me for missing Sunday school. Mom exhaustively tries to convince otherwise to no avail. Baby brother Tommy pulls up with stick horse. We ride off into the sunset. Beware. God punishes bad girls.

Standing obediently in the corner, face to the wall, for committing some unknown offense. All three-year-olds should know better. Wondering about this world and how to get out. Parents are God, they know everything, and they make all the rules. There is no escape. But there must be something else, another way, there just has to be, there just has to be. Please let it be so. Please. Please. I have to pee.

When Michael, the oldest, was about three years old, he stuffed French fries into the car's cigarette lighter. Dad seriously informed Mom that Michael would no longer be permitted to ride in their only car. When Cathy and Michael were about five and seven, he decided that they should remove all the debris from the yard one cold bleak winter morning. They were told that they would get a lick of Formula 44, his heavy leather belt, for every piece of paper they missed. Upon inspection, he dug under blades of grass to find minute pieces of paper or foil, and counted each one as a hit. Both were given several whacks for not doing their jobs as he'd instructed.

Dad forced all the kids to watch when anyone was given a beating until we figured out how to hide. From the very beginning, our fear of our father loomed heavily in our lives. It was he who decided how things should be and ruled as the absolute law of our world.

⟨⟩

Dad never told the story about their elopement in front of Mom. And she never spoke of their wedding, except to say that their marriage was not recognized in the eyes of the Catholic Church. Dad wanted us to be raised in his church, Methodist, *and* the Catholic Church. The Catholic Church said no, so our parents said no to the Catholic Church, and we were raised Methodist.

I suspect Mom must have thought that by marrying, she would escape the oppression of her own mother's home. By all indications, Mom's mother had been born pissed off. Nothing had ever happened or ever would to change that disposition. Every year on her birthday, through all of Mom's growing up years, Grandma gave an account of the particular dreadfulness and excruciating pain of her labor while giving birth to Mom. In return, Mom frequently favored us with the story throughout our childhood, in such acute detail that I can still hear the words verbatim, although it's beginning to fade . . . slightly. Dad turned out to be in some ways quite similar to Grandma, and he beat us kids with a leather belt like just like his father had beaten him. His fits of rage and sudden violence scared the living shit out of every one of us.

Mom was frightened of him too, although he never once laid a hand on her. She told us many times as we grew older that she wanted to leave him but was too afraid. And she had no idea how she'd ever be able to support the five of us on her own.

We weren't poor and never wanted for the necessities of life, but there wasn't much extra money, especially when we were young. Dad liked the controlling aspects of keeping Mom on an allowance that wasn't quite enough to buy groceries and all the things we needed. As a salesman for a large welding supply company, he spent a great deal of his time traveling. Mom, a full-time housewife with four little kids to care for, was not allowed to work outside of the home—just like Dad's mother. Along with how children should be raised, Dad had definite ideas about women and their place in this world.

My father believed that it was okay for a woman to be college educated (even though he was not, which was immaterial because he was above it all) but only as an adornment and accolade to her husband and his career. You might say we were his property to do with as he wished. Property that he loved, but property just the same. Mom came home one day with her long hair trimmed a few inches more than usual and, when he angrily complained about it, she defiantly made sure to have it all cut off the next time.

Mom always possessed a true artistic talent; she was an excellent cook, baker, housekeeper, seamstress, and decorator. She loved sewing clothes for Cathy and me while we were growing up, including original one-of-a-kind Halloween costumes each year, and she even made curtains for our home. She taught us all how to ice skate, roller skate, swim, do crafts, and so many other fun activities. She read all of the childhood classics to us as we listened intently in a cluster around her, imagining what it would be like to be one of the kids in those stories, like the ones who lived in a boxcar.

Over the years she was president of the Garden Club, was active in the PTA, and had us in the Brownies, Girl Scouts, and Boy Scouts. She accomplished all of this and more in a dress and high heels, and with a body like Marilyn Monroe's and the face of a goddess. Mom ran circles around any Martha Stewart-type that ever existed, and she did it on a tight leash and a tight allowance, while married to an obese, drug-addicted, controlling, violent, physically and mentally abusive male chauvinist.

Every week, with our nickel allowance burning a hole in our pockets, we would race down the sidewalk as fast as our little legs would carry us to the local general store. On the front counter by the cash register were large glass jars filled with various assortments of brightly colored penny candies. Mr. Petrunger, the owner, carefully placed our selections into small brown paper bags, which we gratefully collected as we ran out to a place where we'd devour our sugary treats, leaving the door swinging shut behind us.

That store was in the center of the small, quaint country town of McKean, Pennsylvania, where we moved shortly after I was born. It is located in the far northwestern corner of the state where the winters are long, cold, and bitter. Mom made our little white two-story house into a home. We spent hours on the huge swing set that Dad built for us in the fenced backyard, and digging, digging, digging in our boat sandbox that attracted and entertained all the neighborhood kids too. Somehow we accumulated a small menagerie of pets that we loved and were a daily part of our lives, in and out of doors. One below-zero winter morning, Michael was saddened to find Thumper, his rabbit, frozen stiff dead in its cage. He recovered pretty well, because the following spring he begged Mom to please please pleeease let him dig up its skeleton and take it to school for show-and-tell.

In winter, against stern warnings, we sucked on icicles we'd broken off the house, made snowmen and snow forts, and went sledding on toboggans and round silver discs. We built forts made of blankets in the house. We drank hot chocolate and ate scrambled eggs and warm buttered toast sprinkled with sugar and cinnamon for breakfast and peanut butter and jelly or fried bologna sandwiches for lunch. For dinner we feasted on fish sticks, pot

roast, liver, mashed potatoes, green beans, carrots, spinach, apple-
sauce, sliced white bread, and pork chops.

Mom always managed to scrimp and save and pull off the
most beautiful holidays. Christmastime was like a fairy tale every
year growing up. For weeks we were gently assaulted by the sweet
aroma of pine needles that filled the air during that holiday season
along with the charming happy vision of a tree strewn with colored
lights, its branches weighted heavily with candy canes, ornaments
of every shape, size, and color, and globs of tinfoil icicles, standing
slightly askew in the midst of brightly wrapped packages, ribbons
and bows, tricycles and toy trucks. There was always at least one
branch somewhere near the bottom, where only the youngest and
smallest of us could reach, which was overloaded with at least
twenty too many ornaments.

On Christmas morning a plate and empty glass sat on a nearby
table with a special note left by Santa, who must have been the one
who had drunk the milk and eaten Mom's famous butterball cookies we had left out the night before. Our Christmas stockings were
hung with care down the staircase railing, filled to overflowing
with Life Savers, chocolate Santas, and other treats. It was a dream
come true, that one day of the year, so long anticipated that our joy
was nearly uncontrollable, causing us to scramble out of bed and
charge down the stairs, all legs, elbows, and flannel pajamas.
Unbeknownst to us, on a few occasions we arrived literally on the
heels of Santa's boots, much to his dismay.

In the summer we made mud pies and played tag and hide-
and-seek. We rode tricycles and pulled a wagon with wooden-
slatted sides, strewn with prize rocks, up and down the cement
sidewalks from one end of town to the other. We crawled on the
roof of the little red schoolhouse, getting buzzed by hornets.
Scrapes, cuts, bruises, tears, dried tears, peals of laughter. We peed
and pooped behind the bushes at the church. We played doctor

with the neighborhood kids. I taught school to Tommy, the cats, and my doll babies. We dreamed of growing up to become cowboys and cowgirls.

For two weeks each summer we attended Bible School. We drank grape Kool-Aid poured from big, dented aluminum pitchers into jewel-colored aluminum cups, leaving colored mustaches. We went swimming and played in the sand at family picnics on the lake. We rubbed dandelions on our arms, turning our skin yellow. The big kids chased us, caught us, and rubbed the hairs on our arms until we cried. On hot, sticky summer nights, we caught lightning bugs in jars with holes in the lids. In the fall, we walked to school, carved pumpkins, and went trick-or-treating with brown paper grocery bags.

Always we lived in fear of Formula 44, Dad's leather belt, nicknamed after a popular cough syrup and also a reference to Dad's large waist size. He was so big he couldn't buy clothes in a regular men's department. He was eventually prescribed drugs to help him lose weight, which never happened. The diet pills kept him awake, so he was also prescribed tranquilizers so he could sleep. There were migraine headaches and back pain to deal with, and the older we grew, the more pills he took. And this was just the beginning.

CHAPTER FOUR

In the middle of 1964, with all of us except Michael still in grade
school, our family moved to Erie, Pennsylvania, a big city com-
pared to McKean. Our new home was a modern one-story brick
ranch house located in a pleasant little cul-de-sac. Shortly after we
moved in, Tommy and I realized through buckets of tears that our
huge red plastic piggy banks that we had been saving our money in
for all the years we had been alive were missing. Dad had secretly
given the movers our piggy banks as payment.

Dad became so compulsively and obsessively neat in the new
house that he hit us with his belt for each mark we might have
accidentally made on the freshly painted walls of our new home.
He constantly policed us and made sure that we all understood that
the house was to be kept in perfect condition. There was no room
for error. Discipline was a prevalent gloom that could sink the
brightest day without warning. Early one weekend morning, Tommy
came into the bedroom I shared with Cathy singing, "Sucker,
sucker, fucker, fucker," and so I joined in with him singing, "Sucker,
sucker, fucker, fucker."

Suddenly, Dad came barreling like a madman down the hall
toward our room in his huge underwear, clutching Formula 44 in
his hand. He jerked his head for us to come out into the kitchen,
where we bent over and he hit us several times, leaving raised,

bluish-red welts on our small little butts bleeding through thin pajama bottoms. He never said a word. Not knowing why we had been punished, Cathy finally informed us that *fucker* was a bad word. It would be a very long time before I would say that word again . . . I think it was just last week.

Once a week, after our nightly baths, we'd race into the family room, skidding on the carpet and landing in front of the television to watch our new favorite shows, *Bewitched* and *Get Smart*. My cowgirl dream became a little more refined. Bewitched, atop a pretty palomino, wearing a little black dress and heart-shaped diamond pendant, with cowgirl boots and hat. Perhaps that is still the dream.

Dad's parents lived in Erie and we visited them on holidays at their spotlessly clean and orderly house, which always smelled of cooking and Dove soap. Dad's younger sister, knock-out Aunt Carol, occasionally swooped by with her built-like-a-brick-shit-house body, beehive hairdo, latest-fashion dress, and heels, to admire and lavish attention upon us before dancing and twisting the night away somewhere with her current boyfriend. Dad also had a younger brother, a year older than Michael, who had been born blue when his umbilical cord wrapped around his neck and cut off the oxygen to his brain.

When I was about seven years old, this creepy teenaged uncle, who had up until then ignored my very existence, lured me into his room to show me some magazines with pictures of naked women. Then he took me into the dark garage. He tricked me by lifting me up onto a windowsill and slid his hand up the leg of my shorts, inserting a finger into my vagina. When I ran out, Cathy ran to get Dad, who wanted to beat the hell out of him but was stopped by our grandfather.

The incident was never again discussed; it was over and done with as far as everyone else was concerned. I was not even vaguely aware of what he had done to me, but I was left feeling deeply ashamed and confused for many years. I felt certain that I must have done something wrong. Why had this happened to me? If only I hadn't gone into his room, if only I hadn't gone into the garage with him. If only, if only, if only . . .

After two years of living in Erie, Dad was promoted and we moved to Charlotte, North Carolina, into a nice big two-story house with plenty of room in a neighborhood with lots of kids. It was the best time of our childhood for four reasons. Dad was gone a lot, Mom was less stressed, the sun was always shining, and Bill lived across the street. We became best friends. He made me laugh like no one else, except maybe my sister Cathy. With mild winters and long warm months in between, we were outdoors much of the time. Our days were filled with the whirr of our roller skate wheels upon the pavement of the street, running as fast as we could, hiding while playing tag, and playing kickball. We walked to school through the woods each day and every spring the beautiful dogwood trees would cover the ground with their delicate, white flower petals, transforming it into an enchanted magical forest that just might be filled with fairies.

The mid-sixties were in full swing, and The Monkees were big. (I still hear "Daydream Believer" in my head.) Like every other young girl, I had an enormous crush on Davy Jones. Bill's older sister attended a Monkees concert and came home with a piece of a paper cup he had drunk from and thrown into the crowd of screaming teenage girls. She reverently thumb-tacked the scrap to her bulletin board. It was a big deal, and I was lucky because Bill would take me into her room to see the bulletin board. We were not allowed to actually touch it, so we would just stand there and admire it, while occasionally smiling at each other.

Two short years later, we were disappointed to find out that we were moving to Akron, Ohio. We loved Charlotte and we didn't want to leave our home and our friends. Many years later, we'd learn that Dad had been demoted. It was the middle of the winter. We went from a bright, sunny place one day to a dark, dreary, cold city the next. Each week we scrambled for the best seat to watch *Rowan and Martin's Laugh-In* and *Happy Days* for some much-needed comedy relief. Nearly every day, Dad came home early from work and plopped down in his favorite recliner in the family room, sadly and quietly sitting and sleeping the time away. By then, Michael had developed a nasty habit of beating the shit out of us whenever our parents went out. He was a big kid, and even us other three kids together were no match for him. These beatings went on for several years, since we were all too afraid of what Dad would do to Michael if we told.

There was big, crazy excitement one day when Michael was run off the sidewalk by a car full of crazy, drunken teenaged kids. I don't think Michael was hurt too badly, but Dad went out to where the kids lived and blew a hole through their engine block with a handgun in the middle of the night. It was strange how Dad could be so protective of us. The problem was that no one was protecting us from *him*. His "protection" never instilled a sense of safety in me; in fact, it made me more afraid of everything. As I grew older, Dad told me that if a man ever harmed Mom, my sister, or me, he wouldn't report it to the police. He would take matters into his own hands, and that man would disappear from the face of the Earth, never to be heard from again. I believed him.

Less than a year later we moved back to Erie, because Dad was fired from his job at the company where he'd been employed since we were small. All we knew was that he had an impressive new job as a welding engineer for American Sterilizer. He talked about how this job would normally only be given to a college graduate, but because of his knowledge and experience, he was hired. Dad's drug abuse continued unchecked, but he still functioned. Little by little, the veneer of our family portrait was beginning to crack.

We moved into a brand-spanking-new house with red aluminum siding that had just been built in a modern suburban housing development in a "good school district" and a "good part of town." So we were told. It didn't matter to us, but it seemed real important to Dad. We would have been just as happy back in McKean. This would be the home where we would stay until we were old enough to leave, and this would be the house where Dad would die alone and desolate in his bed at the age of fifty-five.

From a certain direction our house was the last house on the left. There was a popular horror movie out at the time, *The Last House on the Left.* I never saw it, but I recall being struck by the coincidence. It was here, while living in this house, that the most traumatic and deeply wounding events of my life would take place. All of our lives would crash, leaving us silently reeling with nowhere to turn, forever altered and rearranged. My worst self-destructive behaviors and thoughts would take root here, leading me into adulthood rich in the follies of madness. All this and more happened while we lived in the last house on the left.

— CHAPTER FIVE —

I was now attending my fifth elementary school. Once a week, my new sixth-grade class would watch a program on educational television about interesting people and places. One week not long after I arrived, members of the Peace Corps appeared on the show, discussing their assignments abroad. At the end of the program we were invited to write a letter to the station if we had any questions about the show. A few weeks later our teacher, Miss Presta, was mysteriously called out of the room during class. She returned with a huge smile on her face as she announced that a student who'd written the station inquiring about the Peace Corps had been invited to be a guest on the show. She asked if we knew who it was. I turned and looked around, craning my neck to see who'd raise his or her hand, but no one did. When Miss Presta called out my name, I couldn't believe it.

She told me that I'd need to prepare several questions to ask a panel of Peace Corps members, along with another student of my choice. Of course, I picked Scott, the cutest boy in the class. Mom and Dad proudly escorted me to the television station, all of us in our Sunday best, me in a dress and black patent leather shoes, white anklet socks, and all. It was the middle of winter, and I was so cold I shivered and hugged my arms around my too-skinny, too-tall, awkward self. Scott and I and the Peace Corps members were seated around a large conference table and as the cameras rolled we asked our questions. I was especially shy, nervous, and exceedingly relieved when it was all over. Still, the experience was very thrilling and the highlight of my academic career to that point.

Erie was where Dad planted four fruit trees in the front yard of our big new corner lot, one for each of his four children. We ate turkey, mashed potatoes, and stuffing for Christmas and Thanksgiving dinners and ham on New Year's and Easter. As always, everything looked fine on the outside to our new neighbors—we were just another family—but inside Dad's rage continued to hold us hostage.

My older brother Michael grew into an out-of-control teenager. Our new house soon became a war zone, with Dad and his eldest son constantly going at it, head to head like two stubborn bulls. Tommy and I dove under an end table in the living room one night when a fight broke out. We huddled in our pajamas with our eyes squeezed shut, our arms around each other and heads down as we heard the sounds of Michael being beaten. Mom tried to intervene, but she was either too late or too helpless to stop it. The beating came to a devastating end when Dad knocked Michael's front teeth so far in they had to be removed.

It was all hush-hush, but the next day we noticed that Dad had a bandage across the knuckles of his right hand. Sometime later Michael popped out his four front teeth, showing us they were false, but never saying any more about what had happened. At the age of eighteen, Michael graduated from high school, got a job, and moved in with Frances, our maternal grandmother. Our house became incredibly calm overnight, though I felt an air of invisible sadness with him gone.

His problems followed Michael over to Grandma's house. After many years of mental and physical abuse, he had grown into an angry and troubled adult who was impossible to control. Soon after he moved out, Michael met a girl. They married. Soon they were in their own place as he tried his best to be a husband. For a short time, Michael and his new bride were happy, but it didn't last. It couldn't. Michael continued to abuse drugs while maintaining a full-time job as a welder in a local shop after his divorce. He'd already begun to use heroin and hang out with known drug users and dealers.

Jim, our father, was a large, heavy man known as Big Jim. Over the years my sister Cathy shortened his name to BJ, then Beej, and that is what we all called him from that point on. Beej was still quite an intimidating figure, especially to the boys who came around to see Cathy and me. One night Cathy was sleeping on the front porch with Tommy when some boys from school came by for a non-parental-approved visit. One of them stretched out on the glider with his hands behind his head, eyes shut. Acting super-cool, he very casually said to no one in particular, "Let me know if the old man comes out." Seemingly out of nowhere, a deep, low voice emerged from a miniscule crack in the front door, booming, "I'm letting you know." Those boys nearly jumped out of their skin, shooting like rockets out of there, faster than anything we'd ever seen.

Beej was really strange about boys being with Cathy and me. He drilled it into our heads for years that men only wanted one thing from us, and that was sex. I didn't really grasp what he was saying until years later. In school they had shown us some ancient short film, and all I could remember about it was a drawing of an antelope-looking thing that had little eggs coming out of it, which was supposed to be a depiction of the female reproductive system. It was far from the whole story, and the lecture that followed was sadly lacking any further answers or clarification. What were they talking about and why were they talking about it? Why were the boys excluded? What was all the secrecy and the aura of shame surrounding it all? Why did Beej go so crazy about boys? Was this the eighth wonder and mystery of the world? Like many before and after me, that short class and Beej's warnings were the sum total of my sex education.

It was 1970. I was thirteen and in the eighth grade. I was just on the verge of womanhood; I had budding breasts and I had recently begun menstruating. I was still very much an innocent girl dreaming of becoming a woman. I had no idea what sexual intercourse was or how women became pregnant.

I started hanging out with a girl named Lucy, the sister of the man whom Cathy would marry one day. We were all stealing booze from our parents' cabinets and had already been drunk a couple of times. A nearby church hosted dances every Saturday night, which Lucy and I enjoyed because it was one of the few things girls our age were allowed to do on our own. One night I met a boy there from another junior high named Kevin, and I immediately liked him. I didn't know much about boys or romance, but I was innocently hoping that he liked me back.

One night, Lucy and I made plans to go to the weekly dance together. She stole a bottle of gin from her parents' house that we'd hidden in my house. Mom and Tommy dropped me off in front of the church. I smuggled the whole fifth of gin, wrapped in my light blue thin nylon jacket, into the dance. I don't remember why, but unfortunately Lucy was a no-show. I started drinking the gin straight from the bottle.

When Kevin, the boy I liked, arrived, he found me sitting on the sidewalk in front of the church. I'd drunk so much gin that my head was spinning. From that point on the night became a fragmented blur. Kevin leaving, then returning, asking me to come with him, leading me by the hand to a small wooded place between the church and the neighborhood houses. Me lying there, boys standing around me, five or maybe six of them. Kevin and these boys I don't know raping me one after the other.

I don't know what is happening. I want it to stop. Full-out, bloodcurdling screaming at the top of my lungs, but they keep raping me. Am I screaming out loud or in my head? I do not know. Maybe I could not scream out loud, and that is why they kept raping me. They thought I wanted them to rape me. That is why I will never be able to tell anyone, because this is my fault. Because if I'd been able to scream out loud or run or tell them to stop, they would have stopped. Wouldn't they?

I was a thirteen-year-old virgin, lying in a patch of poison ivy and being repeatedly raped, and Kevin directed every moment. He gathered the boys together and waited while they each took their turn on top of me. I don't remember how it ended. I have a vague memory of Mom driving me home, but I didn't tell her what had happened.

The next morning, I woke up with blood-stained underwear and a raging case of poison ivy all over my legs and my arms, which became so infected with pain and oozing that I ended up with scars. I tried to hide it, but thankfully, Mom finally noticed and provided me with prescribed medication. I told Lucy about the rape and made her swear not to tell another living soul; she immediately told Cathy, but that was all. The two of us never spoke of the rape again. Cathy and I never spoke of it at all. She was just as paralyzed into silence as I was, and no adult was ever told.

I never told either of my parents, because I was scared and in my mind it was my fault. Once again, I didn't fully understand what had happened to me. I couldn't believe or comprehend that this boy, whom I'd had no reason to mistrust, had done this to me. I thought that I must have deserved it for being there alone and because I drank the alcohol. I thought I was the one who'd done something wrong. If only I hadn't been there alone, if only I hadn't drunk the gin, if only I hadn't walked back into the secluded area.

If only I had run, or screamed out loud, or told them to stop. If only, if only, if only . . .

I felt paralyzed by fear, guilt, and shame. At only thirteen years old, already I was damaged beyond repair and would never feel or be good enough, ever again. I was permanently broken and would never be loved by anyone, ever. My innocence had been stolen and my perception of life had been altered, and I had no idea how deeply and darkly it would color my world from that moment on. The repercussions from that night would haunt me for many years to come.

Nor did I have any clue how to handle what had happened to me. So I did nothing. I remained mute about what had happened, along with the many questions I had about how and why this boy had done this to me. I gradually buried all of it. I pretended that nothing had happened. I was like a wounded baby bird that was grounded, unable to fly but still able to function and breathe and carry on with a life that was less. I'd always remember the anniversary of the rape, because it coincided with Mom's birthday in May. Why? Why? Why?

— CHAPTER SIX —

Fortunately, I didn't become pregnant, and my poison ivy eventually healed. Yet the scars were permanently on my legs and inside my soul. I was sure that these boys told other kids what had happened that night, especially when we all attended the same high school. All during high school, I felt that my classmates talked about me and judged me behind my back. That gave me reason enough to hate school and bide my time until I could escape. The shame I felt was thick and unshakable, and I wore it everywhere.

After the rape, if a boy initiated sex with me, I let him do it. Afterward I hated myself for allowing it to happen. One night I was out with Lucy, and some boys brought us to one of their houses. We all hung out in the basement and one boy, who was a couple of years older than his friends, asked me to give him oral sex. I didn't want to do it. He tried to persuade me. I was able to refuse and he finally left me alone. But that night was unusual. Many times, I would go along and give the boys—and later, the men—what they wanted, which was very rarely what I wanted. What I wanted was insignificant to me, and so it was to others as well.

The doorbell rang. Lucy stood on our front porch with a fresh black eye, compliments of her father. She was running away from home and wanted to know if I'd go with her. Needing no coaxing, I hastily agreed. I didn't know what I wanted, but I was pretty sure there had to be something better out there. We hitchhiked to a nearby college and ended up in a dorm, spending the day smoking dope and drinking wine with a group of older boys who lived there—until one of them found out we were only twelve and thirteen and became scared that they could be in deep shit. The next thing we knew, the party came to a screeching halt when Lucy's brother Jake pulled up to the dorm like a police car in pursuit of dangerous criminals, with our fathers as passengers. Oh shit! By the look on Beej's face, I knew that the consequences of this event would be harsh and long-lasting.

Lucy and I hadn't even been gone overnight, but the incident shook my parents up pretty badly. They thought Lucy and I together were an unsafe combination. My parents made me go to see a psychiatrist. I had no say in the matter; an appointment was set and I was driven to it and seen by the doctor. He asked me a few questions about my family and if I liked animals, my sister, and my brothers; then he let me leave. I must have answered him acceptably because I never had to go back. I could no more confide in the psychiatrist than I could in any other adult, because my trust had long since been shattered. Shortly after this escapade, Lucy moved to Florida with her family, and that was the end of our dangerous liaison.

My two closest girlfriends from seventh through eleventh grades didn't graduate from high school and, at separate times, were both hospitalized for attempted suicide. By seventh or eighth grade, the three of us were already sniffing paint thinner from a rag until we passed out. We abused any drug that was available to us: alcohol, LSD, marijuana, mescaline. A couple of times we each swallowed an entire package of over-the-counter carsickness pills that left us totally incoherent and just plain fucked-up for twelve hours at a time. I never liked the hard drugs much, because they made me feel too out of control. I only used them on several occasions and stuck mainly with alcohol and pot. My friends' parents weren't strict like my parents; they let us smoke cigarettes at their houses. I spent many weekends sleeping over with my friends throughout my teen years. We camped out in the basement, spinning 45s, dancing, and talking about boys, smoking, doing drugs, and drinking.

The rooms of my family's house became increasingly disorganized and cluttered with papers, books, and magazines. Beej became obsessed with going to garage sales and collecting things to sell at his own world's biggest garage sale. At one point he went on a hamster cage-buying binge, and I told Mom that I wished he'd build a rocket out of the cages and blast off to the moon. But he never did. The once spotless and organized basement, as well as the two-car garage and eventually the entire house, became filled with his junk. Up until then, all of our other homes had been neat and clean. This house was not, and only became worse as time went on. Beej's mind was deteriorating along with the state of our home.

A few years after we moved to Erie, Beej mysteriously left American Sterilizer. Later, after he died, I would find the "pink slip" from when he was fired. At the time, of course, we were not told anything. All I knew was that he'd gone back to iron-working and other odd jobs here and there. He was unable to secure another white-collar job like that ever again.

I was distracted from my troubles at home by what seemed to me almost a miracle. At the end of the ninth grade, Chris, a boy from school, became my first real boyfriend. He was very popular; all the girls were crazy about him. I couldn't believe that he was even interested in me, much less wanted to be my boyfriend. I was afraid that he might've heard about the rape. I eventually told him about it and when I did he gently consoled me. He said that he'd heard rumors that other girls we knew from school had similar experiences with some of the same boys that I named. If there were others who were raped they never reported the incidents either, at least that we knew of.

The doorbell rang. I answered and there stood a uniformed policeman asking questions about my little brother Tommy. Sensing that something was very wrong, Mom came to the door, and then Cathy joined us too. "Is this where Thomas McNabb lives? Ma'am, your son has fallen into Walnut Creek and we are searching for him."

In June 1972, Hurricane Agnes had swept through Erie, causing our gentle, shallow Walnut Creek to turn into raging rapids ten feet deep. Tommy had been forbidden to go there by Mom and Beej. He went anyhow, when he found a boy to join him after all his other buddies said no. We learned they had tied ropes around their waists and gone cliff-climbing. Tommy fell in. The other boy went for help.

Mom and I screamed and started to cry as Cathy grabbed the car keys and drove to the creek to see what she could find out, hoping against hope like the rest of us that Tommy had managed to climb out somewhere and was lying in the woods, waiting to be rescued. They searched for him all night. There were scuba divers, riders on horseback, and helicopters.

We cannot believe what is happening. Friends and family fill our home. We wait, and wait, and wait, for the longest eighteen hours of our lives. It is like being picked up and dropped into a bottomless pit, then free-falling in pitch-black darkness with nothing to grab onto or land on. No one sleeps.

Early the next morning, I was upstairs listening to the news on the radio while Cathy was lying on the family room floor listening to the news on the television. We heard them announce that the body of Thomas McNabb had been found. That was how our family was informed of my brother's death. We heard horrible screams coming from Mom and Beej's room. Nothing would ever be even close to right, ever again.

He'd been trapped by a fallen tree, which prevented him from being swept into Lake Erie. The police told us that we were lucky that he was found at all. It was the worst day of our family's life, and lucky wasn't an emotion that we could even remotely feel. From that day forward and for many years, I wanted to die. There are no words to describe how it felt to lose Tommy. He was only thirteen years old. We buried him in his blue suit, with one of his stuffed bunnies and his warm comforter. Beej had A MUCH LOVED BOY engraved on his grave marker. This was the first time I'd ever seen him cry.

Beej explained to Cathy how his death was especially bad because he was a male child. It was all so devastating. Our parents were beside themselves with grief; we all were. After the funeral, we didn't talk about it. Nothing would ever be the same. His room was left alone. His toys and clothes would still be there seventeen years later when Beej died and we had to clean the house out to sell it.

Everyone loved Tommy. He was so pure, sweet, and innocent. When he was swept away, what was left of our family's innocence was swept away with him. It was as if he were too good for this world, and that is why he left. I was still numb and in shock from the rape. When my little brother drowned, I made a pact with myself that I wouldn't love anyone good ever again, to ensure that I would never be hurt in that way, ever again. Unconsciously, I began building a cement wall around my heart that would eventually close me off from the opportunity to love and be loved by anyone good. Because those you love die.

Our family fell to pieces, too many pieces to ever put back together. I felt grateful that, at least, Tommy had escaped from our childhood. I wished with everything I had that there were some way for me to join him wherever he was. I often prayed for that to happen, but it never did. It would be many years before a day would go by that I didn't cry or think about him. He had been my best friend in the entire world for as long as I could remember.

The following Thanksgiving, I found a school art project in the dining room buffet drawer that Tommy had made out of colored construction paper for Thanksgiving. In crayon, he'd drawn a turkey and listed all the things for which he was thankful; mostly he was thankful to be alive. I cried. Tommy died, but before he died, he lived, and the day would come many years later when I'd remember that. The silent invisible air of sadness that filled our home became impossibly thick and heavy, like sticky flypaper, keeping us trapped in a web of grief that is probably still there.

My boyfriend Chris became like another son to our parents. Beej hired him to do the yardwork and they did things together just like he and Tommy had done. Chris's parents really liked me. Before we met he'd been running with a seriously bad crowd that had stolen a car, and he had already been in trouble with the law. As soon as we met, all that behavior ended. He lived with his father; his mother lived nearby, married to a man who really loved Chris. Sometimes, before he had his driver's license, when they went out, we'd borrow his mom's car and drive around town.

We had sex as often as I'd let him. We were in love, we were each other's first love, and that was all that mattered. We wanted to stay together forever, so he tried to make me pregnant; it didn't work. Thank God. As far as I knew my parents were not aware that we were having sex like rabbits. The subject was never discussed.

Many times, Chris's older sister would bribe us with a bottle of Boones Farm Apple wine to baby-sit her kids. We came of age getting drunk on cheap wine, listening to Heart of Gold, Neil Young, Leonard Cohen, Cat Stevens, and Crosby, Stills, Nash, and Young. Chris loved playing the guitar, and these were the artists who inspired him. And, of course, we all loved George Carlin and his *Seven Dirtiest Words* album too. As we entered the tenth grade, Chris's parents helped him get his first car, a VW Bug. His stepfather was an older, wealthy man who owned a restaurant and liked to drink. Sometimes when we visited them, his mom would pour bottles of booze down the drain, cursing him.

In a fit of anger one evening after dinner, she sketched a picture of his uncircumcised penis for us. Chris pleaded, "Mom, Mom, no, no!" But that didn't stop her. She was a trip. She was very beautiful, with coal-black hair and blue eyes like Chris. She was very young-looking, always wearing miniskirts at a time when no one her age wore miniskirts. But she pulled it off very well.

When fall came, we entered high school and a crazy time. Between classes, there was always a rush of girls who congregated in the restroom, loudly talking and laughing while puffing away on cigarettes, leaving the space empty and quiet just as quickly as we'd entered. Some enterprising student had knocked the back out of a locker, making a great place to hang out while getting high and smoking. One girlfriend, Cindy, had a brand-new red Camaro that a bunch of us would cram into and go tearing over to McDonald's with the stereo speakers blaring full blast. My sister Cathy, who worked there, would give us two huge bags of hamburgers, cheeseburgers, and fries. We smoked cigarettes and joints the whole way there and the whole way back as we stuffed burgers and fries into our faces. With all the smoke, the speeding, and squealing of tires, I don't know how Cindy could even drive or why we never got caught. The next year our school was professionally monitored and we couldn't do most of those things anymore. But for a while, it was wild.

I'd sometimes look up to see Kevin, the boy who had raped me, walking by me in between classes, but we never spoke. We'd pass each other in the hall as if nothing had happened, making sure to steer clear of each other. There was another boy whom I also occasionally passed by and recognized from the rape, but he never acknowledged me either. Seeing them only brought up the feeling that something was broken inside of me that could never be fixed, a feeling that I didn't want to think about. I'd never have thought to actually say anything, maintaining my silence. After all, it was my fault. I must not have been screaming out loud. I didn't stop them. I must have wanted it.

Beej rejoined Masterweld, the company he'd started with his father years before. A few months later, his father died suddenly of an aneurysm of the heart. This was almost more than Beej could bear. If he'd been on a downhill slide before, this only made it worse. Our grandfather had not made any provisions for Beej in the will, and the business went to our grandmother and his brother. Eventually, the business went bankrupt. It must have been worth some money, because our grandmother lived for over twenty more years on what was left to her. After some time had passed, our uncle refused to let Beej work at Masterweld any longer. This was a bitter pill for our parents to swallow, but the truth was Beej probably was not able to perform his work due to the drug abuse.

This time in my life marked the beginning of a reoccurring nightmare of being endlessly chased by someone who was going to kill me. I was either running and getting nowhere, or I was so paralyzed by fear that I couldn't move to save myself. I would wake up extremely shaken, anxious, and disturbed. These nightmares became a regular part of my life and would continue for almost three decades. Life was crazy and normal, sometimes at the same time.

44

— CHAPTER SEVEN —

A s first loves generally do, Chris and I gradually grew apart and broke up after the tenth grade. I can still hear Cat Stevens's "Wild World" when I think of him. My first love, my first breakup—I wilted like a dying flower for a time. Chris had come into my life in between the rape and Tommy dying. I don't know what I would have done without him there by my side. I don't think he ever knew how important he was to me in my life and how much he helped me through that most devastatingly difficult time.

In my junior year I went steady with a boy named Mark who was a senior. Like Chris, he was very popular and well liked by the other students. He had hair almost as long as mine, well past his shoulders. We were allowed to drink beer at his house, which was like one big party. He came from a big family with lots of kids. His father was successful in the construction business, and he often arrived home after a few too many drinks, inadvertently parking his big long car diagonally in the driveway. We had a lot of fun together and spent many hours drinking beer, listening to music, and making out on the floor amidst his big, noisy, busy, house full of kids, parents, cooking, television, running, laughing, and scream-ing. Elton John singing "Bennie and the Jets."

I really loved this boy, and he told me he loved me. I wanted to be with him all of the time. I was thrilled and in heaven when he took me to his senior prom, where I wore a beautiful flower-print dress that Mom had bought for me, with my long hair curled and pretty. My older brother Michael, who loved to pull pranks, came by to see us off. He choreographed and snapped a picture of Mark that night in his tuxedo, holding my beloved cat in the air by the tail. I only discovered this incident when I went to the drug-store, picked up the prints, and saw, to my horror, a photo of my cat dangling upside down. Those bastards!

Near the end of the school year, Mark started seeing a senior girl behind my back. I was devastated when he broke up with me one afternoon; some of our friends and his new girlfriend were in the other room. It took me forever to get over him. I drove home through a veil of tears listening to Aaron Neville's "Everybody Plays the Fool" on the car radio.

～

As soon as my sister Cathy graduated from high school, she moved to Florida with her best friend Josie. The first time I visited, I was very impressed with my big sister's apartment, which had cost them all of twenty-five dollars to furnish with goods from the Salvation Army. They drank from glasses taken from local bars; a napkin holder from Dunkin Donuts was my favorite. They had a construction horse with a flashing light in the living room and a street sign on the wall. It was the coolest place I'd ever seen.

My girlfriends and I made many spring break road trips down to the beaches and bars over the next few years, often making the twenty-four-hour drive straight through by taking amphetamines to stay awake, flashing the truck drivers our bare tits and singing along to Beatles tunes on the radio the whole way.

When we arrived we would hang at the pool or drive an hour over to the famed Daytona Beach. It was the early seventies and there were clubs throughout Florida called Big Daddies. The one in Daytona was huge, four or five stories high. During spring break each floor featured a different live band and dance floor, all of them packed to the rafters with drunk, screaming kids just like us. One standing-room-only night, Cathy lit a joint right inside and we smoked it. No one seemed to notice or bothered to say a word to us. Cathy was always pushing the envelope, and I was right there by her side. We swayed to "Hey Jude."

During one of my visits, I met Larry, one of Cathy's co-workers. My sister was spending most of her time with her boyfriend Archie or working, and I was free to run amok. Larry, who was a good twenty years older than I was, offered to show me around. We ended up back at his place having sex. I wasn't at all into having sex with him, but I did like hanging out, drinking, and getting high free of any curfews, rules, or parents, so I pretended to be into the sex. Cathy didn't like what I was doing, and we had a few heated words about my behavior that ended just short of a brawl. If our parents had known what I was doing, I would have been in a ton of trouble. After a couple weeks of staying out all night and drinking, I reluctantly returned home to parents and curfews.

Josie eventually tired of Florida and moved back home to Erie, so Cathy and Archie moved in together. Needless to say, our parents did not approve. The live-ins came to Erie for a visit, and Cathy brought him home to meet our parents. Larry, the older man I'd met, accompanied them. He invited me to move to Florida and live with him once I graduated from high school. I wasn't too keen on that idea; fortunately for me, soon after their visit he got some other girl pregnant and had to marry her. In the meantime, at home in Erie, our parents were beside themselves with worry over the situation with Cathy, as well as with this older Larry guy.

It wasn't until years later that I saw a picture of myself with this man, taken during that visit, and truly realized what a creepy letch he really was. No wonder my parents were so alarmed. He'd preyed on me, but I was too naïve to realize it. Cathy had known, but was powerless to stop it. It was a very long, uncomfortable visit. My parents were somewhat mollified when later that year Cathy and Archie returned to Erie to be married. The wedding was a happy but brief occasion for our family, providing us with the chance to see some relatives we hadn't seen for a while. On her visit home Cathy and I watched silently out the kitchen window into the backyard while Beej replaced Tommy's fruit tree. It had mysteriously died not long after he did.

∽

Chris and I remained close. The summer before my senior year, I was over at his house one night with two school friends, Cindy and Kevin. We'd drunk a case of pilfered beer and smoked a few joints. After we were all pretty loaded, Cindy and I went upstairs and returned stripped naked. We didn't have to convince the boys to join us, as they fell all over themselves ripping their clothes off and followed us to the car. We all hopped in Chris's VW Bug, threw our clothes in, and tore down the road with Neil Young serenading us as we headed toward a couple of parties to streak the night away. First stop prep/villa party, the private high schools where all the rich kids went.

The four of us ran through the house, totally naked, laughing uncontrollably the whole way. The prep boys didn't like it and thundered toward us, angry enough to beat the shit out of us by the time we'd run through the whole house and raced back outside to the driveway. Kevin ran into me and knocked me over in the confusion. He pulled me up by one hand as Chris yanked me up by the other in the opposite direction, just as the prep boys were closing in. It was a close getaway; we barely made it to the car, got it started, and sped away as the boys chased us.

We headed to another party and, along the way, thought it would be funny to stop and pick up a hitchhiker we saw on the side of the road. He turned out to be a boy from school, and he must have been on LSD because he totally freaked out. We tried talking to him, but he wouldn't talk to us. He just kept staring blankly ahead, telling us to let him out. He'd known all of us for years, but he just kept telling us to let him out. I guess all the nudity was too much for him. We dropped him off at a bar, got out of the car, ran around a little, and peeled off into the darkness, laughing in the warm summer night.

We headed to a party at the apartment of some older kids from my sister's class. When we knocked on the door, one guy opened it and let us in. We ran in through the apartment, all the way back to the kitchen, planning to exit through the back door, but it was completely blocked by cases of empty beer bottles. We had to turn around and go back through the apartment to get out. One guy looked at us as we ran into the kitchen, passed out, and crashed to the floor as we whizzed back toward the front door. The same guy who'd opened the front door was still standing there holding it open, and he watched with a smile on his face as we flew by him.

We ran to our car, jumped in, and sped away, screeching the tires as we fled. We laughed until our guts ached. In the car we finally put our clothes back on, while Chris drove us home. None of our parents ever knew what we'd done except Chris's mom. She was only disappointed that we didn't streak through their elegant restaurant!

Later that summer, I began hanging out with Josie, Cathy's best friend, who was back in town. I was sixteen, turning seventeen in August, just before my senior year of high school. She was nineteen.

The two of us started going out to bars using fake IDs. For one hundred and fifty dollars Beej had bought me a 1964 Chevrolet Belair that was Earl Shieb turquoise blue with rust marks. Josie's car was nicer, so she usually drove whenever we went out. She was seeing a local policeman who was much older, and married besides. He had a partner, and one night she wanted me to sit in the car with him while she spent some time with her married boyfriend. I definitely didn't want to, but she managed to talk me into it.

We met the policemen at some secluded place. The partner, Slick, quickly climbed into Josie's car with me, a big, sinister grin on his face. Slick was about fourteen years older than me. He was overweight, balding, and reminded me of someone's father, or worse. We talked until Josie got back into the car. I certainly wasn't attracted to him: he was gross. As we drove away, Josie said they wanted us to meet them later, when they were through with their shift. At the appointed time we drove to the police station and waited for them in a nearby parking lot. Before I knew what was happening, Josie left with her friend, leaving me alone with Slick in his car. He gave me some confiscated beer, taken from a citizen by an on-duty police officer. He stole it from the police department to give to me, a sixteen-year-old girl.

Slick immediately started putting his hands all over me and trying to kiss me. I tried to push him away, but he was much bigger and stronger than I, and very determined. He got his hands down my pants, and touched me insistently. I started to like how it felt. No boy had ever made me feel that way before. He pushed and pushed until he was having intercourse with me. I told him no over and over, and I tried to get away from him, but his size and strength gave him complete control over me. He took my clothes off, then his pants. He refused to let up and finally forced his erect penis into my vagina. He sweated profusely during sex and dripped all over me, including my face. He gave me my first orgasm.

I continued to see him. He gave me more orgasms. Other than regular meetings in public at the donut shop (how clichéd) while he was on-duty, he rarely spent any time with me, except to have sex. He always promised we would do something together; then, at the last minute, he either cancelled or didn't show up. He told me he loved me. I convinced myself that I loved him back. I learned that he was married, had two daughters, and was expecting a third.

Slick told me that he would leave his wife and marry me when I graduated from high school, and I believed him. All my life, I'd thought that I was supposed to grow up, get married, and have children. Our relationship was sick, crazy, and chaotic, but I went along with it. I didn't know what normal was, and didn't know enough to be the least bit interested in finding out. My parents knew nothing about the relationship. If they had, Beej most assuredly would have done something that would have significantly altered the path of all our destinies.

Josie and I met up with these cops many times. They gave us money to buy beer, took us to bars where they knew someone, and arranged for us to buy beer since we were both underage. Sometimes they met us at bars and bought drinks for us all night long. They'd buy the pizza, and we'd have what they called "rendezvous" with them, which also happened to be the name of a neighborhood bar where we often met and were allowed to drink. When Josie and I arrived, they'd have the hood of the police cruiser open, with the pizza in the box sitting on the engine to keep it warm.

It was possible that this may not have been the first time that these two pillars of the community had done this, and it probably wasn't the last. Yes, they were having a good time on the taxpayers' money. Of course, at the time, it all seemed very thrilling and glamorous to two teenage girls, except the sex part. That was something else entirely and was not at all glamorous.

In my senior year, Beej found me a 1972 Mustang convertible. Buying that car was one of the nicest things he'd ever done for me. He spent a long time locating that car and then haggling over the price—they probably sold him the car just to get rid of him. My new car was blue with a white top and beautiful. The car loan was in my name, and I paid for my own insurance. I was on an early work release program from school and found a job at Sears as a sales clerk.

Every weekend (and sometimes during the week) I went out with Josie or some of my classmates to dance and drink at one of the bars or after-hours clubs that allowed underage girls to slip in. I became friendly with two classmates, Claudia and Sally, and we became constant companions. We had fake IDs but usually weren't asked to show them. Every one of us drank and drove, but now that I had a nicer car than most of my friends I was usually the one stuck driving. Our excessive drinking, dancing, and driving was wild, dangerous, and a normal part of our lives.

Slick, too, remained a dangerous and normal part of my life. I was constantly breaking up with him, and he was constantly lying to me and leading me on. I soon learned that he was screwing anyone in a skirt who would lie still long enough. Still, he was very possessive of me and a couple of times became physically abusive when he found me out at a bar talking to other guys. I did my best to stay away from him, but he would find me in his car, convince me to get in for a few minutes, and talk me into seeing him again. This man was an expert; he really knew how to manipulate me into allowing him back into my life over and over again. He had a way of making me feel hugely sorry for him. If that didn't work, he gave me money and sometimes bought me gifts. But that was rare. Mostly he manipulated me and that worked quite well for him since I was naïve, gullible, and easily misled.

The worst part of the whole affair was how much I hated myself for enjoying sex with this repulsive man. I alienated myself from friends my own age by spending all my free time around him. During my senior year of high school I was so embroiled with him that I didn't date any boys my own age and missed the chance to attend my senior prom.

Slick's wife's sister was in my class, and when his baby boy was born she talked about it at school, showing off pictures of her new nephew in the girl's room. Every time I broke up with him and thought that he was finally going to leave me alone he started to chase me again. He was absolutely relentless in his pursuit of me.

I never used any form of birth control and, in due course, I became pregnant with Slick's child. The day after I graduated from high school in June of 1975, just two months shy of my eighteenth birthday, Slick whisked me over the state line to New York, where abortion was legal. "(You're) Having My Baby," by Paul Anka, was playing on the radio in the doctor's office while I waited for the drugs to take effect so that the abortion could be performed. Slick arranged and handled everything very quickly. I went along with it because I did not know what else to do. I couldn't imagine facing my parents with this news—not in a million years. It was over before I really knew what I'd done. My parents had no clue about Slick or the abortion. It was one of the saddest days of my life. I felt so utterly alone.

I thought of just a few days before, when one of my maternal, hands-folded-neatly-in-her-lap great-aunts had said to me upon my graduation, "This is the best time of your life. Everything is downhill from here." I thought to myself, *I hope she's wrong; otherwise I really am screwed over. Totally and completely.*

Chapter Eight

Somehow the authorities discovered that Beej had been seeing several different doctors and using different pharmacies to obtain excessive amounts of drugs for years. When the local narcotics agent investigated Beej, no charges were filed because it was concluded that he wasn't selling drugs, only using them. Beej started getting into serious automobile accidents as he slipped further and further into drug addiction. During a harsh winter storm the phone rang in the middle of the night. A state trooper was on the other end, asking if we knew where Beej was, because his car had been found abandoned along the side of the road with the door left wide open. We were scared. The police eventually found him unharmed. From that point on, every time he walked out the door, we didn't know if we'd ever see him again.

Beej taught welding at a tech school for a short time after leaving Masterweld. One day I noticed that he'd forgotten his lunch, so I took it to him. When I found his classroom, he was in front of the class teaching and let me in when he saw me. He was clearly happy to see me, judging by the smile on his face, and he tried to introduce me to his students. But he staggered and was stooped over, stumbling over the words like he had a mouth full of grapes. I could hardly hold back my tears as I handed him his lunch. There he was—forty years old but looking sixty, the skin hanging slack from his face and neck, all pale and gray, like a sick dead fish. Cheap drugstore glasses magnified eyes hugely out of proportion to his face, and his clothes were a little dirty and worn.

I remembered the sharp, crisp, clean-white-shirt-suit-and-tie-shiny-shoes-blue-eyed handsome dad of my youth—where had he gone? Where was my big strong dad with all the answers, all the power? Could he really have been reduced to this impotent, lack-luster caricature of a human being? Once I was in my car I let the tears fall, thinking about all the years I'd watched Beej slowly destroy himself. It was not easy to watch one of my parents, one I'd loved, feared, and admired my whole life, fall. To see through the pretense and finally face the truth of his larger-than-life fatal flaw was another devastating moment in the life of the child of a deeply disturbed and troubled man. If he who was my universe is weak and frail and knows not how to live, then what chance had I?

I continued to live with my parents after graduation. I also continued to drink heavily. After working as a waitress for the first year after high school, I halfheartedly thought it was time to get serious about a career. So I went to work at the home office of a large insurance company. I worked my way up from filing to underwriting to a position as a claims facilitator. I often went to lunch with a co-worker, Charlie, who was one of the claims adjusters. He used to pull out his flask from under the front seat of his company car as we pulled out of the parking lot, and we'd pass it back and forth all the way to the restaurant. Then we'd drink throughout lunch and drink more on the ride back, returning to the office and the afternoon ahead smashed.

One night I met a man named Bill at a party, to whom I was very attracted. The feeling was mutual, and we started seeing each other. I was twenty and he was thirty-eight, but he looked more like he was in his late twenties and was drop-dead, gorgeous hand-some. He was the first man to wine and dine me—nice restaurants, good food, fun times. He had a really great sense of humor on top of it all. I was so insecure; this man was really too mature and sophisticated for me. I'd find out later that he really was another low-life-hound packaged in good clothes and good looks.

I drank and stayed out till all hours; it wasn't long before Beej took notice and tried to curtail my activities. He was concerned about me "getting into trouble" (oooops . . . too late!). Little did he know I was already in so much trouble it would take me more than two decades to climb out of the hole into which I'd fallen. He told me to get out of the house, but Mom said I didn't have to move if I didn't want to. I was ready for my freedom but afraid of being on my own. And I was worried about the future of my parents.

Mom, who by this time was selling real estate, found me a little townhouse to buy. She helped me pick out wallpaper and hung it for me. Beej helped me paint and did some electrical work for me. They gave me an old living room set that had been sitting in the basement for years, and I bought the rest of my furniture dirt cheap from an estate sale. It was really nicely furnished for my first place and would still be very nice even now. I continued working at the insurance company, and also took on another job at a fancy country club as a hostess. I had to work two jobs to pay the mortgage, the down payment, and my car payment, along with normal living expenses. I was just starting out and I was already overextended. I'd repeat this pattern over and over like a broken record.

I was still seeing Bill off and on when Slick the cop tracked me down and came over to see my new place. He offered to fit a piece of carpet into my bathroom while I was at work, asking for a key. We hadn't seen each other for a while, and he was trying to weasel his way back into my life. One night Bill and I went out, returning afterward to my place for the night. Slick must have been parked nearby waiting for me. He unlocked the front door with his key, ran up the stairs, turned on the bedroom light, and there we were *in flagrante delicto.* I saw Slick turn off the light, then bolt down the stairs and out the front door. Bill grabbed me and dove off the other side of the bed, onto the floor for cover. Lying there naked and tangled together in the sheets, he asked if that had been my cop, telling me he'd never be able to get another hard-on again as long as he lived.

Bill was involved in some nefarious business dealings and outright illegal activities, including a high-stakes poker game. He'd already seen the police cruiser at his apartment complex and was well aware that I'd been involved with a cop. Not long after this incident—and after somehow managing to recover long enough to get at least one last hard-on—Bill broke it off with me. I continued to sporadically see Slick the cop. I couldn't get him out of my life.

My wisdom teeth became infected and impacted, so I scheduled to have them removed at the hospital. I was to be put under anesthesia and spend one night at the same hospital where I'd been born and where my maternal grandmother worked as a nurse's aide. It just so happened that I was scheduled to stay on her floor. After surgery, I started coming out of the anesthesia and found myself in the elevator on a gurney. A hospital orderly was standing over me, and I suddenly felt his hand under my hospital gown on my bare skin, fondling my breasts. I was very groggy and unable to move, but let out a startled gasp when I realized what was happening. He looked me in the eyes and realized that I'd awakened. He pulled his hand out from under my gown and acted like nothing was wrong. The doors to the elevator opened and he rolled me to my room. He transferred me to my hospital bed as Mom, who was there on the other side of the bed, helped him. He was real nice and friendly, joking around.

As soon as he left I told Mom what he'd done, and she said not to tell anyone. She didn't want to upset my grandmother. I wanted to report him, not only for me but because I knew he'd do this to others, but I deferred to Mom's judgment. Years later, when I asked Mom why she didn't report this incident, she said that she did what she considered to be best for me at the time. She felt that reporting the molestation would have been a difficult ordeal and did not want to put me through that process.

I had been violated once again. As a young woman this experience, on top of the others, only deepened my shame and guilt, leaving me confused and angry. My deep inner rage was steadily building and would continue to fester, occasionally surfacing. I'd watched my father lose his temper and inflict violence upon us (especially Michael and Cathy) many times over the years, and I'd sworn from a very early age to never lose my temper and hurt others the way he had. Instead, I turned my anger and rage inward toward myself. This caused deep depression to develop within me that seemed to become a part of who I was, a condition I thought must be accepted but never welcomed. The depression frequently and easily turned my mind to thoughts of suicide. Alcohol was my medicine, temporarily relieving me of the deep sadness that sat like a million little stones inside the chambers of my lost and broken heart, which I couldn't shake out no matter how hard I tried.

The insurance company where I worked produced its own monthly magazine, which was distributed to employees and policyholders. One month they did a feature on women on the rise in our company, a "climbing-the-corporate-ladder" kind of story. I was interviewed for the article, along with another woman who was higher up in the company. Our picture appeared on the front cover. Outwardly, my life appeared to be happy and successful.

By the time I reached the legal drinking age of twenty-one, I'd been living a hardscrabble life for years. I'd been going out to bars for five years, drinking for nine, abusing many other drugs, and smoking cigarettes and pot for just as long. I'd been gang-raped, molested twice, and physically abused as a child, and my little brother had died. I was promiscuous, and had had sex with a married policeman followed by an abortion. My thoughts, attitudes, decisions, behavioral patterns, and actions all flowed like invisible blood from the psychic wounds of my childhood traumas. I felt completely alone in the world, with no one to help or protect me. I knew there would never be anyone that I could trust. My life had always felt this way, for as long as I could remember.

And this was just the beginning.

— PART TWO —

She paints inside her soul
Visions we cannot see
Swallowed up whole
In a world we can't possibly know,
She dreams . . .
Madness dances across her soul,
She paints a not so pretty picture . . . ,

Come with me on a flash of a mind I used to call my own,
Don't blink, 'cause you may miss it
The pain and intensity of a corrupt soul

She sees a child in her head, skinny and frail
Her life, a punishment for sins she never committed
She battles inside a child who never wore childhood
The child wants to come out and play but it's too late
She doesn't understand.
The thinking becomes intense
She wants to break in two.
The pain becomes her main focus now
Her soul will never forgive her.

Her insides are raw and empty.
So consumed by visions of memories from the past and glimpses into
the future of what she is afraid to become.
She has already given up so much in life.
Insanity and madness is all she now knows.
Something we cannot even begin to imagine.
Her eyes stare blankly . . . too young to be so far away.
I reach out to help the stranger I once knew so well.
I try and touch her fear, hoping to ease the pain.

But it's useless.
Madness dances across her soul
She paints a not so pretty picture . . .

—Sarah M. Montesi

— Chapter Nine —

My one true dream for as long as I could recall was to be a homemaker. Since that career seemed unavailable to me, I settled and did what I had to do in order to survive. I inquired about the position of automobile and homeowner claims adjuster. I was told that there was no room for me at the home office because they'd already filled their quota of "women adjusters." I'd have to be willing to move to a branch office. So I decided to transfer to the Canton, Ohio, branch office.

A really nice man from the home office, whom I'd met while working at the country club, was instrumental in helping me get the new job. When I proudly and excitedly told Beej about my promotion, he warned me that the man who had helped me was after something. That deflated my joy; I was left feeling demeaned, like getting the job had nothing to do with my abilities. While Beej was wrong about the man who'd helped me, there was another man who did have an unsavory agenda. One of our claims supervisors made a drunken pass at me after a company picnic, which I turned down. Men in supervisory positions pursuing me for sex would become another reoccurring pattern in my life. I cowered from unwanted attention and advances made by men I didn't know, or barely knew. I purposely wore little or no makeup and wore clothes that hid my figure. As a naïve, frightened, and easily intimidated young woman, I barely knew what I was doing half the time, let alone how to fight off unwanted advances by employers.

I was scared to move away from Erie and my family. I didn't know what Mom would say, but she was supportive of the move. If she hadn't been, I might have stayed in Erie. I rented my cute little house to my druggie roommate and her boyfriend, and the insurance company paid for my move. Maybe I'd escape all the bad things that had happened to me and all the bad things I'd done.

It was the late seventies when I moved to the small town of Alliance, south of Canton, Ohio. I was determined to start a new life in my modern new one-bedroom apartment. I was given a brand-new company car, a raise, and an expense account. I'd finally escaped Slick the cop once and for all. My past was behind me. Maybe life would be better now. I thought that if I could move a few hours away from home and survive on my own, later I'd be able to move even farther. The farther away I moved the better it would be, except for one teeny-tiny little problem. No matter where I lived, life didn't get any better.

This move was the beginning of approximately fifty moves within at least ten states, twenty-something cities, and numerous and various apartments, jobs, friends, and men. This first move to Canton was the beginning of my trying to outrun myself. No matter how far I ran, even to the most remote place on Earth, it would never be quite far enough. It was exhausting trying to outrun myself, but I was young and driven by something dark and deep within me. Once I started, I couldn't stop running to save my life.

I drove back home to Erie every weekend because I didn't know anyone in Ohio. It was a three-hour drive that became old quite quickly. Mom and Dad were preparing to split after twenty-seven years of marriage. Dad did not want Mom to leave, and probably felt that way until his dying day. We represented the best parts of his life and now it was all slipping away. Beej told me that it was my fault they were splitting up. Could it have had even a little something to do with his being a drug addict most of his adult life? Could it have been that he was totally screwed up, living in his huge underwear and, evidently, by the smell of him, liberated from the need to bathe regularly? He was so far out of touch with reality by this time that in his mind the demise of his marriage was my fault. He turned really ugly toward me. I didn't defend myself because I knew he was out of his mind. That night I turned to walk down the stairs leading to the laundry as he came to the head of the stairs, yelling and calling me a tramp. That was a new low, even for him. It was the worst thing he or anyone ever said to me.

Back in my new apartment in Alliance, I had a nightmare in which Mom was wearing a conspicuously bright, hot-pink outfit, and I was trying to get to her because she was in danger. I called home the next morning, very concerned, and told her about the nightmare. She said everything was fine. A couple of weeks later Mom called me and told me that she had been sitting in the kitchen talking on the phone with Ben, a longtime friend of the family, when she heard a gunshot fired from the family room. Beej had shot the big stuffed chair in which she usually sat with a .357 Magnum handgun, probably the same one he had used to blow a hole in the car engine years ago. Ben told her to put the phone down and leave the house while he called the police. The entire SWAT team showed up. Beej surrendered and was taken away to the mental ward of a local hospital. Ben was there by then and said that he'd remove the gun from our home. After the police left, Ben and Mom discovered enough loaded weapons underneath the couch to wipe out the whole SWAT team, as well as the entire neighborhood.

This was in the years before the Betty Ford Center, rehabs, and interventions. Mental wards of the local hospitals were where people were sent for drug abuse treatment. Beej was under strict watch—no razors or anything sharp near him. When I went to see him I tried not to cry. The nightmare of my real life just kept getting worse. Beej was originally required to stay for a few weeks, but almost immediately outsmarted the doctors and was released early. He was back home doing drugs again in no time. I don't know what he told the doctors, but he told me that he'd been shooting at an evil eye with teeth. The bullet went clean through a huge over-stuffed chair and the sliding glass door, which he never bothered to replace. Ben held on to his guns for several months, and then returned them unloaded.

There were times when I thought if he died, then all of the madness would end and I would be relieved. I felt deeply guilty for having those thoughts. It would take another ten years before he did die. A long ten years of wondering which phone call it would be, knowing that it was only a matter of time.

Mom waited until Beej was on his feet and working steadily again before she finally left him. I saw him only a few times during those last ten years of his life and only spoke to him over the phone on a handful of other occasions. He disowned me for a while over the divorce. When I did see him the air surrounding him was so thick with sadness and despair that it was palpable and almost impossible to bear. I already had a problem with depression and thoughts of suicide. I needed a push in the other direction. Poor Beej had one hell of a bad time. This was not his turn to have a happy life.

Meanwhile, I was doing well working for the insurance company in Ohio. I drove to a nearby city and started working on the weekends at a bar instead of going home to Erie every weekend. My former roommate and her boyfriend trashed my precious little house before they broke up and moved out. I sold it after the next tenant proved that he could destroy my property in ways even the others hadn't thought of.

I worked at the bar for about a year, pounding down vodka and shots all night long—from seven or eight in the evening until two in the morning. I had an affair with one of the married bartenders that fizzled out after several months. I continued my promiscuity as a means to end my loneliness and fill up the deep chasm of painful sadness that defined and ruled me. Hopeful fucking. Maybe he'd be the one to fix me and love me. I continued to work for the insurance company during the week and the bar on the weekends.

At one point I was sent to my hometown for a two-week claims adjuster training class. Adjusters from all seven branch offices also attended. It was so boring I had to fight to stay awake. One night before going back home, a bunch of us spent most of the night drinking and dancing in the hotel bar. We made a silly bet about jumping in the pool—it was the middle of winter and freezing cold. When some guy named Earl and I lost the bet, we jumped into the pool fully clothed. Then we went to his room to dry off and started making out like a couple of monkeys in heat. The next day in class I was so hung over I thought I'd pass out, making a big commotion as I sprawled out on the floor in front of the class, and maybe even vomiting on our instructor's shiny black shoes. Fortunately, it was the last day of class.

Back in Ohio, a guy I barely knew asked me to marry him. We hadn't even so much as kissed, and I couldn't take him seriously. Suddenly, nothing was working for me anymore. I walked out one night in the middle of my shift at the bar where I'd been working and then quit the job at the insurance company, which I'd become bored with while fighting depression. Some days I was barely able to crawl out of bed. Cathy had just given birth to her first baby, and we both thought it would be a good idea for me to move to Florida to be near them. I'd worked for the insurance company for four years, the longest I would work at any one place during my life.

Driving into Florida, I felt like I'd entered another world. One day you could be in freezing temperatures and the next you were walking down the sidewalk lined with orange trees wearing a light T-shirt and shorts. I stayed with Cathy, her husband, and my niece, until I was able to get a job and move into my own place. Before long, Cathy introduced me to Jack, a guy about my age with whom she worked. The first time we met at a party, looking into his eyes as we shook hands, I immediately felt that this man was not a good person for me. That was not something that had ever happened to me before, and rarely since then. Jack and I ended up in a bar drinking shots. We did a lot of shots in those days, and even I could only tolerate so much alcohol.

Jack gave me a ride home and I graciously thanked him by vomiting all over the inside of his brand-new Corvette. The next day he called me and wanted to see me again. Of course I ignored that small voice that said, *No Linda, no don't do it!!! Pleeease don't do it!*

We went out a few times and then he invited me to spend the weekend at his parents' beach house. He'd just graduated from college and was on a management fast-track training program at one of the large grocery store chains. His father was the president of the company or something. They were quite wealthy, at least by my standards. Jack told me he was serious about finding a wife and had plans to someday honeymoon in Hawaii. I was in my early twenties and this all seemed promising, except for the bad feeling in the pit of my stomach. I was excited to be spending a whole weekend with him because we hadn't spent any time together; he was always cutting our dates short for one reason or another. I couldn't figure it out; you would have thought he was married or something.

We got an early start and drove to the beach about an hour or so away. The beach house was beautiful and it was right on the ocean. We spent the day on the beach, and I was planning to make dinner when he sprung it on me. He'd invited his best friend to join us. I couldn't believe it. This was really odd. Who invites a friend on a romantic weekend for two? I was very upset about this, but I tried to play it down. When it was time for bed, he and I went into one room and his friend into another. Jack and I made love. We'd already been intimate a couple of times before. I was really into it, but he was not. He acted like it was a chore for him, and I didn't understand. Until I met Jack, I usually had the opposite problem.

After we were finished making love, he hurriedly said that he was going to go see his friend. He explained how he rarely got to see him and they just wanted to spend a little time together. It was the middle of the night! I was never stupid, but I was certainly gullible. It turned out that the friend was his lover and he was using me as a cover. He was living a secret life. I didn't see that at the time, nor had I ever had any prior experience with this type of situation. Not long after, Jack abruptly broke off our relationship. I was crushed.

I moved out of Cathy's and into my own apartment in a senior citizen condominium community. I didn't live there long, because I was evicted for late-night parties and skinny-dipping in the huge Olympic-size swimming pool. The straw that broke the camel's back was when my old friend Claudia's boyfriend, Bob, was caught urinating on my neighbor's sliding glass doors. It was duly noted that the woman who turned him in had spent a significant amount of time examining the offending member. Claudia, whom I knew from high school, ended up renting a little house together with me in the College Park area. Sally, another former classmate who was getting divorced and living in Florida, began hanging out and partying with us.

I started dating Josh, a friend of Claudia's boyfriend. We all had nine-to-five jobs, and the minute we got off work—especially on Fridays—we'd start getting stoned and drinking beer. They had some kind of killer weed that made me pass out. Josh and his friends all had boats and sometimes we'd go to the river or have cookouts. It seems to me that we had a lot of fun, but my memory is not clear because we were always so loaded.

I worked at another insurance company as an inside claims adjuster and was eventually promoted to claims supervisor. There was a loud-mouthed obnoxious bitch posing as a woman who thought she should've been the one to be promoted. She often bad-mouthed me to others and tried to make my life a miserable hell. She did a pretty good job of it too. All day she sipped from a can of soda spiked with vodka. One night I went out with her and a bunch of other women to a club, where the entertainment was an all-male strip show. We were all seated on couches waiting for the show to begin when one of the older ladies took a vibrator out of her purse. She highly recommended that we buy one to pleasure ourselves. Later I'd realize the wisdom of that recommendation.

After I'd been working at the insurance company for a few months, I started calling in sick. Often I was still high from the night before, dropping the phone on the hardwood floor and fumbling around for a good long time before finally getting it up to my ear and slurring that I would not be coming into work that day. Amazingly enough, I was not fired from that job. Life was filled with drinking, vomiting, getting high, passing out, eating, working, hangovers, skinny-dipping, dancing, sex, and, on the good days, spending time with my niece.

Once we were all in the car headed to another bar when Claudia and Sally, who were in the front seat, turned around just in time to see me vomit into my hands and throw it out the car window. We just kept right on partying, going to another bar, and drinking more. We were always up to something when we were out. One time we pulled over to pick up a car door in the yard of a body shop; we took it on tour to Cathy's house in the middle of the night, then home again to place it in Claudia's bedroom, where it became a part of the décor.

The house we shared had no central heating or insulation, making it quite frigid in the wintertime. Many a night I'd come home to find that Bob had built a roaring fire in our wood-burning fireplace, where we sometimes roasted hot dogs and marshmallows. I'd find out later that he was tearing out pieces of wood from the garage behind the house to build those fires. By the time we all moved out, it must have been ready to collapse. Once he brought over a chain saw and tried to cut down one of the trees in our yard but stopped when the tree was not easily felled. He was afraid our landlord, who lived next door, would catch him in the act. He left an enormous gouge mark in the tree trunk.

We were inspired by a Cheech and Chong album to roll a foot-long joint and smoke it. The floors of our house were all wood and pretty indestructible, so we tossed our empty beer bottles and cans on the floor when we partied. Sometimes we liked to drag the kitchen table and chairs out to the driveway and bring the party outside. Cathy, Sally, Claudia, and I went often to Sunday brunches to drink champagne while taking Quaaludes. On one of the Sundays, Sally and I sat there and discussed Claudia's drinking problem while getting smashed ourselves. We had to laugh at the irony—we were well aware that we were drunks too, but that never stopped us.

Something in me was still restless and desperately sad. I became terribly bored with my job and even though it appeared I was having fun, I knew that drinking and getting high was not what I really wanted out of life. I knew I wanted more but had no idea how to get more. I felt stuck and in a dead-end situation. My solution was to keep running. I decided to join my mother in a new life in Dallas, Texas.

CHAPTER TEN

To the enormous relief of my supervisor, I quit my job and made the move to Dallas, Texas. The early eighties Dallas atmosphere was thick with materialism: cosmopolitan big-haired women wearing diamonds and gold, perfectly manicured hands pulling out thick wads of hundred-dollar bills at the cosmetic counters of expensive department stores; Jaguar, Mercedes, and lime-green and purple Rolls-Royce valet parking reservations; everything expensive, everything for sale; pine trees on the top floor of buildings under construction; cars crammed bumper to bumper on too-small highways; rush hour, happy hour; Coors beer swimming pools; cowboy hats, boots, the Dallas Cowboy cheerleaders, and football players; tennis courts, mansions, oil money, JR, Sue Ellen, Jock, Miss Ellie; bars, clubs, restaurants, Nieman Marcus; Pink Floyd's "Money."

Dallas was booming; it was *the* place to be in the early eighties. I joined Mom, who was making a fresh start after her divorce from Beej a year earlier. We both had high hopes for new opportunities and new lives. I worked for a couple more insurance companies before breaking into outside sales and marketing. I moved from one fancy apartment to another, buying clothes and furniture on credit, racking up a mountain of debt, and driving around in the most expensive little sports cars I could buy. I worked the nine-to-five

grind and spent my nights and weekends club-hopping, dancing, drinking, sunbathing, socializing poolside, more drinking, shopping at Bloomingdale's and Saks Fifth Avenue.

Pay the rent or buy another outfit: five-inch high heels and soft, supple, expensive leather handbags? Clearly the outfit, shoes, and handbag. Unblended scotch, Wild Turkey, Jack Daniels, shots with ice water back, drinking to get drunk, hangovers, cocaine, pot. Jumping into cars with strangers in the middle of traffic, driving away, lines of cocaine, all night. More hopeful fucking in a sea of dickweeds.

I was in my mid-twenties and had thought I'd have a husband and a family by now. I loved making a home, cleaning, cooking, baking, shopping, and decorating—and I was very good at it too. I thought I wanted children, but a good partner was first and foremost. And that was not happening. The majority of the men I became involved with were troubled, flat, colorless, and vacant—much like my expectations of life. Thoughts of suicide were never far away.

I met and made friends with a woman named Darlene, who lived in the same apartment complex and had recently moved to Dallas from Ohio. She was twenty-nine and had been divorced three times. She was pretty screwed up, so naturally we became fast friends. We started going out to bars together, and that is how I met Jerry. Jerry was out with his friend Paul and already hammered when the four of us became acquainted over shots. Jerry took me out to his car to smoke a joint in his brand-new Corvette. He was about four years older than I, had his own successful business, was cute, dressed well, and was very funny.

When the bar closed, I invited everyone back to my apartment for breakfast. Darlene and I went to the store and bought food for breakfast with money that Jerry gave us. I cooked breakfast and Darlene helped. We all sat down to a beautiful breakfast and suddenly Jerry jumped up from the table and ran to the bathroom to vomit. The rest of us ate our breakfast as if nothing were happening. He came back to the table later but couldn't eat. His friend went home with Darlene and they had sex. Jerry stayed, but we did not have sex. Still, I was "way" into him. He had me at the first puke.

In time, I would come to realize that Jerry drank so much he had an ulcer, and vomiting was a normal occurrence. I'd wake up in the morning to him jumping up, yelling "gangway," and running across the bedroom to the bathroom to vomit. Jerry kept me from being involved with him on a full-time basis. I didn't know that he had a long-time girlfriend with whom he was living. When they broke up, he moved in with a male friend, and eventually into his own place. Jerry used to call me when he was out drinking, and I'd meet him and his friends or he'd come over afterward.

I wouldn't let him have sex with me until I'd known him for a few months. Even though he wasn't treating me like a real girlfriend, I allowed him into my life when it was convenient for him. I was deeply in love with him.

AC DC, "Tainted Love"; Aretha Franklin, "I'll Say a Little Prayer."

After Jerry moved in with his friend, he was still distant. He went out drinking nearly every night of the week and was sleeping with a boatload of women, which I pretended wasn't happening. He was self-employed in the equipment leasing business. It was an extremely competitive field, and he worked very hard building his business and earning a bunch of money. Over time, he also blew a bunch of money and became less and less attentive to his business because of his drinking. I tried to get closer to him. I broke things off with him frequently, but he always ended up back in my bed. From the beginning sex was exceptionally pleasurable with him, by far the best I had experienced. Unlike most men I had known, he knew what to do. It was always ladies first with him, a code from which he never wavered. Sex with him was an irresistible magnet that kept pulling us back together, time and time again. He fucked the mascara right off my eyelashes every time. Someone within his circle of friends affectionately called me McNookie, and for a time the nickname stuck.

Jerry's friends liked me, wanting him to be happy and for us to be together, but he couldn't commit to or sustain any kind of a stable relationship with me. My friends and family intensely disliked him. That he was not willing to be in my life full-time only fed my ever-increasing feelings of worthlessness and inadequacy. In between seeing him I met other men and started other relationships that never went anywhere. He was the only one I really wanted to be with.

I continued to have the same reoccurring nightmare from years before, and I was becoming increasingly angry and bitter. When I wasn't turning my anger inward it surfaced unexpectedly, spilling and bubbling out onto others in the form of sharp sarcasm, cruel insults, innuendo, rudeness, complaining, and judgment. It was never pretty. I knew in my heart there was no future with Jerry.

I'd been talking to Cathy about moving to Connecticut, where she'd moved with her husband and children. I'd only seen Cathy's second daughter a couple of times. Both of my nieces were getting older, and I wanted to see them grow up. I packed everything, put it in storage, and headed north. I knew as soon as I was on the road that I wasn't quite ready to permanently leave Dallas behind. I decided to spend the summer in Erie with my grandmother after taking her to visit Cathy and her girls. I worked at a friend's bar and hung out at the beach.

I contacted Sally, who was back in Erie by then, living with her second husband. We regularly went out drinking until all hours, falling off of barstools, trashing restrooms, bending down to pick up dropped car keys, falling over drunk, driving home. During that summer we had our ten-year class reunion, which we attended together. It turned out to be one big drunken free-for-all, pretty much like any other night I spent in a bar. I ran into Kevin, the man who had raped me. We spent some time together, talking for the first time in all those years. He wanted to know how I was. I told him I was okay. Lie. Lie. Lie. The rape was never mentioned.

By this time, Mom had met a man named Howard, to whom she was engaged. When the summer ended, I left Erie and moved back to Dallas, living with them for a couple of months. They were married at a beautiful ceremony followed by a reception. Howard proved to be a good and kind man who over the years would do many good things for our family, like moving my brother Michael to Dallas and giving him a job at his company. I called Jerry to let him know I was back in town. He was happy to hear from me and I began seeing him again.

No Linda, no, don't do it again!!!

I found another job and moved into my own apartment, reclaiming my furniture from storage.

After applying for a number of good sales jobs, I ended up taking a job with a mobile home manufacturer. It was the middle of the summer and none of the model homes that we showed all day long were air-conditioned. Every time we'd walk prospective customers through a home, we'd all come out dripping with sweat and nearly asphyxiated from breathing in all the chemicals that were used in the manufacture of the mobile homes. It was hell, but I desperately needed a job, and that is the only reason I continued to show up each day.

One of the other two salesmen, who was about my age, constantly made it known that he was obsessed with large female breasts. The other, much older than me, secretly told me that he'd be having sex with me sooner or later. The younger guy was peculiar but funny, while the older guy was just plain flat-out creepy.

The manager, a decent sort, gave me a little book called *Think and Grow Rich* by Napoleon Hill. I loved that book; it was the first book I'd read that spoke of a "higher mind." I was well trained and easily sold the homes; the problem was that very few buyers qualified for a loan. I was only paid if I sold something, and the financing was rarely approved. So I was not making any money.

I had a two-bedroom apartment, a car payment, and lots of bills. I was broke and had no idea how I'd make all the payments. My stepsister, Howard's daughter, offered to move in and split the rent for the summer. She said we could work at a topless bar as waitresses. She promised to go with me to and from work so that we would be safe. I was hesitant, but in desperate need of money, I agreed to do it. The job was somewhat acceptable because only the dancers were topless.

On my first night of work I noticed that the atmosphere of the club bristled with anger, desperation, and despair, all of which were just barely glossed over by an abundance of drugs, alcohol, money, fake smiles, vacant eyes, bare tits, and bare asses. I fit right in. It was straight-up: I want what you got, now give it to me and let the games begin. All the while everybody was made to feel that this behavior was as acceptable as high tea on the veranda.

The workers at the club were a subculture of people who worked until two in the morning, partied all night, slept all day, then started the whole thing over again, night after night. They had their own little private society, and unless you were a hard-core lifer you couldn't belong. The dancers were very young, and in time I realized that they were all considered has-beens by their mid-twenties, due to the rough lifestyle they lived and breathed day in and day out. The cocktail waitresses were mostly ex-dancers who were too old to dance anymore, though they were rarely even thirty. After a couple of kids plus the ravages of heavy drug and alcohol abuse, it was what they could do to still earn a buck. They were hard and brutal. If one of them imagined that you had crossed her, you suddenly found yourself in a world of shit.

The air was thick with smoke, the floors vibrated with the ear-deafening music, and it was high drama hustling to sell drinks and earn enough tips to pay the bills. Each night I worked, I couldn't wait for my shift to end. As waitresses, we were at the bottom of the heap in the topless club but were needed to sell the liquor, which was very important. Prostitution was present, but not openly discussed any more than the drug deals that were constantly taking place. I did not become involved in the lifestyle; I mostly came to work and went home afterward, usually alone. Except for one night . . .

After my shift ended, I was invited to go to a "party" with one of the dancers and two guys that she knew. They gave us cocaine and asked us to dance for them. I didn't know how to dance like the professional dancer, but I improvised on top of a coffee table. We were all laughing and having fun. The guys wanted the dancer and me to have sex with each other, but she told them I wasn't into that. The dancer went off with her "boyfriend," and I went to another room and had sex with the other man. I didn't want to, but I was so high on alcohol and cocaine that I just allowed him to do whatever he wanted. It didn't go well, to say the least. The cocaine had an unpleasant numbing effect. You might say the whole scene was the exact opposite of fun. The next day the dancer drove my sad, pathetic self back to my car. I felt that I had reached a new low point as a party girl. Hopeless fucking. Hopeless, hopeful, in the end it was really all the same thing.

After a few more disastrous dead-end dates, including one that ended in a high-speed confrontation with a very tall street sign that got the best of me and claimed the front end of my red Camaro, which I gladly donated to the highway department as I tore away from the scene of the crime, I was finished serving cocktails in high heels and a skimpy outfit. I'd only lasted a few months, but it seemed much longer.

I was hired by a company to sell and lease pagers. We were assigned territories and the job was part salary, part commission. We also had expense accounts, health insurance, and paid holidays. This was definitely a step up. This job was the best one I'd found since moving to Dallas. I earned more money than ever before, and my manager and co-workers were great to work with. A year later, a big company bought them out. I'd done so well in my sales that I was offered a chance to stay on with the new sales force, along with only one or two others. My manager was leaving and asked me to follow him to a store that sold and serviced cellular phones. The benefits and salary were similar, so I went with the manager to the new place.

Eventually, I tired of that job because of the difficult sales quota. Every month I had to start over, and I lived under the daily constant pressure of the sales manager to perform under threat of termination if quotas were not met. I was always near the top in sales, but given the high stress I began dreading each day. I applied at all the big communication companies; many times my lack of a college degree disqualified me, leaving me feeling like an underdog and so inadequate.

I knew that it was unlikely that Jerry would ever be able to make any kind of commitment, but I allowed him to wander in and out of my life. I continued dating men in between, always trying to move on but never being able to. Often he'd call me in the middle of the night needing rescue from some bar. One night, he and one of his drinking buddies were so drunk that they pulled up to a popular Mexican restaurant in his Porsche, somehow pinning the restaurant doors shut. No one could get in or out of the front door. They spent the night in jail for that one.

I was living in a really lovely apartment when I quit my job selling cellular phones. I'd somehow managed to get a loan on a brand-new silver 300ZX, and I loved getting behind the wheel when I was drunk, cranking the stereo full blast, slamming the accelerator to the floor, and running stop signs and red lights all the way home late at night. I was in debt past my eyeballs with no income. I became so desperate that I answered advertisements in the local paper placed by men looking for sex. I had a one-time encounter with one man and an ongoing arrangement with another, both of whom paid me for sex. I prostituted myself to pay my bills for several months. I hated myself for this and could barely stomach being with the man. He paid me one or two thousand dollars at a time, thinking that would cover a few visits, but I always demanded more money, trying to keep my head above water. This caused our business deal to eventually come to an end.

I reassured myself at the time that no one would ever have to know that I'd prostituted myself. But I knew. I was the epitome of the "unhappy hooker." It was probably the lowest point of my life. I never in my wildest imagination dreamed that the day would come when I would write about this in a book, telling the world about one of my deepest shames.

I couldn't face prostituting myself anymore, so I filed for bank-ruptcy. I was buried in debt; I didn't know what else to do after I fell behind for one month, then two months. The amount required just to get caught up was staggering; there was no other way out. The guilt I felt from filing for bankruptcy was debilitating and only added to my inner turmoil, weighing heavily on me for a long time to come. Beej had drilled into me that I was only as good as my word; now my word meant nothing.

In order to make some quick money, I went to work at another topless bar that seemed more like an upscale nightclub—if I over-looked the stages, the dancers, and the nudity. Under the shinier surface, everything was the same as the first club I'd worked at, just cleaner and fancier. I worked with no breaks, four nights a week, once again in high heels and a skimpy outfit for at least eight hours a night. It wasn't any more fun the second time around. I sold my furniture and moved in with Mom and Howard, deciding to finally make the move to Connecticut. I was ashamed to be filing bankruptcy and I was losing my car. I felt like an utter failure.

I'd broken up with Jerry many times during the six years that I'd lived in Dallas, usually by throwing his toothbrush out my front door, which of course really meant nothing except that he'd need a new toothbrush. Since our last split, I hadn't seen him for several months and I thought that we were finally over. I heard that he was involved with someone else. When Jerry found out that I was moving to Connecticut, he started to pursue me. He decided that I was the only one who had really ever loved him, and he wanted to be with me. He asked me to move in with him. I refused. He said that he was thinking about asking to marry me. Jerry had spent all of his money, run his business into the ground, filed for bankruptcy, and was back home living with his parents. Even though he was down on his luck, oddly enough I wasn't put off by his situation. I was, however, concerned.

I asked him if he was willing to get help for his drinking. He was afraid, but he agreed. I seemed to think that my drinking wasn't a serious problem in comparison with his, and that I could stop anytime. Beth, a friend of mine I'd met through Mom, had started me on a path of metaphysical study and spiritual healing. She referred me to a woman who was a spiritual counselor. Jerry was embarrassed when he found out that I'd asked Beth for a referral and backed out of going. So I went in his place. Because I had no car, he drove me to and from the appointments. Jeanette, my counselor, was focused and wise, telling me that one of the reasons I drank so heavily was because I held a lot of anger toward my father.

She helped me begin to forgive him. She was also intuitively aware of the "cement wall" I'd built around my heart when Tommy died, and helped me begin to dissolve it away.

I visited her several times over a period of a few months. She told me that she felt she was counseling some of the people who would be spiritual leaders in fifteen to twenty years, and that I was one of them. Her wisdom remains with me even today. I consider her, along with Beth, to be one of my wisest and greatest spiritual teachers. As the sessions ended, I decided to move away. Jerry had refused to get any help with his drinking, and I was afraid I might end up marrying him if I stayed. As much as I loved him and as self-destructive as I could be, even I couldn't do that to myself. Without Jeanette's help, I would probably not be alive today and certainly would have made other life choices that would have been much to my detriment. I had a long way to go, but at least I'd begun the climb out of the hole I'd been living in all my adult life.

— Chapter Eleven —

M om and Howard helped me out by driving me to Connecticut. Cathy and Archie had divorced after ten years of marriage. Cathy was seeing someone new, and they started a mortgage company together, making money hand over fist due to the fact that interest rates had been lowered for the first time in many years. I had a ready-made job working for their company until Cathy announced out of the blue one day that they planned to close the office and handle the business on their own from home. Shortly after closing the office, they moved to Florida. It was crazy. I had moved to Connecticut specifically to be with Cathy and her girls, and now they were moving. I felt upset and abandoned, but there was nothing I could do to stop them.

I immediately began a job search and was soon hired as a marketing representative by a national car rental company with branches all over the United States. They provided me with a company car, a decent salary, and monetary bonuses. I was elated; this was the best job I'd had in quite a while. My marketing manager, William, showed me the ropes. He told me that if I followed his advice, we'd all make money. So I did, and he was right—we did. No one told me at the time—maybe my bosses didn't want it to go to my head—but we were breaking records with our profits. We were the number-one top revenue producers for several months.

However, there were growing pains. The company was young and growing too fast. Positions were being filled without benefit of experienced or trained personnel. I was promoted to marketing director. I knew the basics of the job, but I knew nothing about managing people. Most of the marketing reps were okay with my being manager, but one man and one woman in the New York market didn't want to be bothered by my efforts to train them, especially as their district was also one of the top revenue producers. These two reps made my managerial position as miserable as they could. They refused to fill out reports correctly, for which the home office held me responsible. I was required to go out on calls with each rep from time to time, and every time I visited their office they complained to their own district manager—a young, twenty-two-year-old man—that seeing me was a waste of time. Once the woman came to a company function dressed in very revealing clothes. The next day, I took her aside and suggested that she wear something more appropriate to future company events. She reported this incident to her district manager, who in turn reported everything to my supervisor.

My social life during this time was hardly exciting. I occasionally went with friends to the movies, or out to eat, or sometimes drinking. I continued to abuse alcohol, but less often. One night I met a man at a bar, went home, and had sex with him. I was lonely and had decided to give the hopeful fucking thing another try. After sex, he was very cold, and I knew there'd be no future contact. He didn't want to pursue anything with a woman who would have sex with a stranger. I went home and cried so loud and for so long I am sure the neighbors must have heard, but I couldn't help it. I didn't care. My pain was intense. I cried not just about that night, but for all that I'd been through. After that night, my sexual relations with men began to diminish, along with my drinking.

I was still able to function and work, though when I visited the home office in Cleveland, Ohio, I made a fool of myself. I was so nervous and lacking in confidence that I came off as arrogant and strange. In reality I was just very intimidated by all those men in suits. I was nearly thirty, wore no makeup, lacked a college education, and had no prior management experience or training. Because of all the money we'd made since I came on board, it was clear these men had expected someone else. I set my problems aside and carried on at work. My life brightened considerably when Cathy ended her post-divorce relationship, put her two daughters on an airplane, and flew them to back to Hartford to live with their father. I invited the girls to stay with me as often as possible.

Shortly after my ill-fated trip to Cleveland, some decisions were made about my future with the car rental company. Our regional manager, Ted, demoted me back down to marketing representative due to my lack of management experience. If I chose to stay on as a rep I'd have to move to Boston. Ted told me that he would provide me with the proper training and promised that if I was willing to learn, I would soon be re-promoted. He told me to take some time off to decide what I wanted to do. I called Jeanette, my spiritual counselor, and followed her advice to stay with the company. I'd surprise the corporate big wheels who were expecting me to quit rather than be demoted. I'd take the demotion and work my way back up!

Ever since I'd been in the corporate world, I'd been regularly given advice, offered platitudes, and forced to set long-term goals that had no meaning to me. Some of the more tired expressions that I heard over and over were, "You don't have to like me to do business with me." "It's nothing personal." "Keep your business and personal life separate." And my personal favorite, "Dress for the position you aspire to be in." Okay, first of all, it's *all* personal; and second, if I'd dressed for the position I aspired to, I would have been wearing a bikini and a big floppy straw hat, sipping margaritas from a giant glass with a little umbrella in it. The position I aspired to be was horizontal, atop a lounge chair on a secluded beach in the Fiji Islands or Tahiti.

Even though I'd been able to get along and often succeed in the whole corporate game for a period of time, I started to think that it was a big scam that I'd accepted in order to survive. The nine-to-five grind always felt like a prison to me. It was always about the money; the work was never fulfilling. It didn't take long for these types of jobs to become boring and something I dreaded. However, I didn't know what else to do so I kept going and made the best of it.

Ted was pleased to hear that I'd accepted his offer, which was an important turning point in my life. Ted became the first positive male role model in my life. He believed in my abilities and assumed the role of my teacher. The company paid for my move to Boston, and I easily became acquainted with my new co-workers and clients.

Just as I was settling into life in a new city, I went to the movies with a girlfriend one night, having no idea that I was about to open the floodgates to a long-buried traumatic event. The movie we saw was *The Accused,* starring Jodie Foster, about a young woman who is gang-raped in a bar. As I watched, the twenty-year-old memories of my own gang-rape rushed to the surface. I started to cry uncontrollably. I could barely sit through the movie as I tried to hide my crying from my new girlfriend. I rushed home as soon as the movie ended, crying the whole way, but relieved to let it all out and not suppress it any longer.

When I got home, I immediately called Jeanette in Dallas and told her the whole story. She asked if I could possibly contact the man who was responsible. When I said maybe, she suggested that I try and advised me on what to say to him. She said to not care what his response was; I was to make this call for me; it had nothing to do with him. Somehow, I was able to obtain Kevin's phone number.

I was filled with nervous energy and felt driven by a higher force to right this wrong within myself when I heard his voice on the other end. I told Kevin that he'd raped me and had invited several others to rape me too. I told him that we had all been damaged as a result of that night. I asked him if he knew that I'd been a virgin who didn't even know what sexual intercourse was. He said, "No." I asked him if he recalled me screaming. He said, "No." I told him that I could still hear myself screaming. I told him that I'd gone to see a movie where a woman was raped in a similar way, and it had been a catalyst for reawakening the memory of my own rape. At no time did he deny raping me. He listened to all I had to say, then asked if I was okay. I told him that I was finally getting help after all these years. I said that I was far from okay, but I was working on it.

I called Jeanette as soon as I hung up the phone, and she told me that as I healed I'd be able to help other women who had also been raped. She introduced the concept that there is always a gift in every seemingly horrible event, and helped me to begin to forgive what had happened. I took a long hot shower and felt like I was really clean for the first time since that night so long ago. I hadn't realized how "dirty" I'd felt all those years. I felt better. The healing had begun, but I still had a long way to go.

After that experience, I was drawn to more of my earliest spiritual teachers. The movie *Out on a Limb* with Shirley MacLaine taught me that my inner voice was real, true, and valuable. The book *I Know Why the Caged Bird Sings* by Maya Angelou taught me to not be ashamed and that it is okay to be openly honest; what happens to us can change us but cannot reduce or diminish us. Marianne Williamson's book *A Return to Love* began to teach me about the most important relationship of all: the one within myself.

In my new Boston territory, I worked closely with Louie, the district manager, who'd been with the company since the beginning but had an attitude problem with corporate and a history of shady dealings. Ted saw the potential in him and wanted to help him get promoted. Despite our best efforts, the branches were not making much money. Some of them were losing money because of a multitude of problems in operations, because the company had simply grown too quickly. We plodded along and did the best we could.

Back in the New York region, some disturbing facts were coming to light. When profits rapidly decreased, corporate investigated, and it was soon discovered that the woman who had disdained my training efforts was having indiscriminate sex with many of her clients. She was also having an affair with the other marketing representative, who was married. Neither of the reps had been doing their jobs, probably from the beginning. Their twenty-two-year-old district manager wasn't such a whiz kid, after all. The offices happened to be in a very busy market, but with business not being properly conducted, it was only a matter of time before the bottom fell out. Both the marketing representatives who'd given me such a hard time were fired.

Louie told me that two owners of the company were coming to Boston to interview me for a regional marketing position. He coached me and encouraged me to buy a new suit and some makeup—very solid advice. My meeting with the owners was brief. Afterward, Louie invited me to lunch with William, the man who'd originally hired and trained me, along with Ted and all the district managers in the region. William ordered a bottle of wine, which was a first! As he poured the wine, he told a story about the time he ran an ad looking for marketing reps in the Connecticut market. A woman had called in to say she was running late and would be arriving by bus. William hung up the phone and shouted to his district manager, "Oh great! Some dingbat just called to say that her car was in the shop, and that she was catching the bus to get here. She probably doesn't even have a car." That story was about me.

William said that he always told his managers that story to demonstrate how determined I was, that I did what I had to do to get there. I also used the same determination in my job every day, and it had showed up in the company as profits and big bonuses for us. We all had a very good laugh. William announced that I was being promoted to marketing director for my region. It was a great day, and a very high point in my life. I'll never forget it. I was told later that the owners personally came to see me as a way to make amends for having been in error. They never apologized or even mentioned the past, but I didn't care. Being re-promoted was all that mattered to me.

Everything in my life seemed to be coming together. An old neighbor of mine from Hartford, Lara, called one night from Arizona, where she now worked as a journalist. She informed me that her cousin Jim was coming to town, and asked if I would mind showing him around. When we met, Jim was instantly taken with me. We had a great time together. After he went back to his home in Northern California, he kept calling me. He pursued me heavily. He was at least several years younger, and I was foolishly flattered by his attention. He invited me to come out to California for New Year's Eve 1989. I'd just returned home and been back at work for a couple of days when the phone rang. It was Mom. "Beej is dead." I burst into tears.

She told me that he'd been receiving daily kidney dialysis and, when he didn't show up for treatment that morning, a policeman broke into his house and found him upstairs in his bed. At age fifty-five, Beej was dead. Officially, his death was listed as heart failure, though no autopsy was performed. From the moment I learned of his death, I had a strong feeling that he died of a drug overdose. Given all those years of drug abuse, it was amazing that his body had lasted as long as it did. I cried for what could have been and what would never be, because his time was up. I knew that he'd lived an entire lifetime of misery and pain so that I wouldn't have to. I knew this is how sometimes a parent loves you: it may not appear to be love, but it truly is.

At home in Erie, looking at him in his casket, I thought, *Well, that's it, it's over; I'll never have the family I'd always hoped for.* The small voice inside of me said, *Yes, you will. Someday you will have your own family. It will be good, and far better than you ever imagined.*

As we departed the funeral home and headed to the cemetery to lower Beej into the ground, Mom reached her arm around me and said, "Only Beej and I could've made such beautiful children as all of you." Once the initial shock had worn off, I realized that I was equally sad and relieved that Beej had died. Watching him slowly kill himself all those years had been a heavy burden for most of my life. Now it was lifted from my shoulders.

I wanted to stay longer and help Cathy clean up Beej's house, but I had to fly to upstate New York to train a new marketing rep. After I returned to Boston, Jim continued to pursue me. He came to Boston to visit again, and we had just as much fun. I thought I was falling for him. In fact, I thought I loved him. When he got back to California, we talked about my moving to California, where I'd wanted to live since I was a teenager. Jim lived near San Francisco, a completely different area from Southern California. What I really wanted was to live near the beach in a warm climate, but at the time California was only a dream. I didn't know much about the northern part of the state.

I inherited a little bit of money from my father's estate. I wanted to use the money to go on a Club Med vacation. Instead, Jim talked me into going on vacation with him. He promised it would be the best vacation I'd ever had: in a beautiful beach house in Southern California. He'd have to work during the day, but I could sunbathe and we'd go out at night. He asked me to send him the money so he could arrange everything, and once I got there, he'd pay his half. It turned out to be the worst vacation of my life.

The beach house in La Jolla was not so great. It was too cold to sun-bathe, and the sky remained overcast the entire time. He had me go to the grocery store and buy groceries for meals. We went out only once, with me spending most of my vacation cooking and cleaning. Jim didn't pay me back for his half of the vacation, because he counted buying the groceries as his fair contribution. What he promised was very different from what actually happened.

Obviously, it was time to transfer to a new position in the San Francisco office so I could receive this kind of treatment on a regular, full-time basis. Even before I left Boston, I knew that I was making a grave error. In addition to having a truck loaded and ready to move five hundred miles away to San Diego immediately upon my arrival in San Francisco, Jim also cheated on me, among other assorted indignities. The move, and the relationship, was a complete and utter disaster from beginning to end. We had less than nothing in common. Six months later, he and my job were over. I was living in New York City in an effort to distance myself from my latest catastrophe. It didn't work, but it was a good try.

Lara hooked me up with Kate, a girlfriend of hers who worked at *Ms.* magazine and lived in Brooklyn. Within a couple of weeks, I found an apartment across the street from Kate's, above an antiques store. I moved in, bought some furniture, and decided to work for an advertising agency through a temporary employment agency. I was assigned to work as a switchboard operator at an international advertising agency in Manhattan. I found out who was in charge of sales, or new business development as they referred to it. I introduced myself. They were considering moving one of the guys over to creative, leaving an opening for which I might be considered, but they were in no hurry to make a decision.

A spectacular New York Thanksgiving and Christmas came and went. In the first snowfall of the season, I strolled with friends through Brooklyn Heights, mingling with sparkling white snowflakes. It felt magical as I looked across the water and watched the cars making their way across the bridge into Manhattan. Twinkling lights, darkness of night, crystal snowflakes, and the city skyline. Winter turned to spring turned to summer. In New York, even on a budget, there was plenty to see and do for little or no money, especially in the summer. New Yorkers are a rich, diverse ethnic mix of people from all over the world, the likes of which I hadn't seen anywhere else. They had a fabulous, eclectic personal style that made living and moving among them a pleasure all its own. You could be floating by the Statue of Liberty on a ferry, or viewing the city from atop the Empire State Building, or walking through Greenwich Village, or be ushered into a basement bar to listen to a new band that simply blows you away.

New York was a great city, but due to the high cost of living, rough if you didn't have a higher-than-average income. Life there started to feel like too much of a struggle. When I asked my grandmother back in my hometown of Erie if I could stay with her until I found a job and a place to live, she said yes. I never thought I'd end up back there, but I was suddenly tired of the big city life. Every day feeling alone and isolated while surrounded by millions of people, fire engines, ambulance sirens, and sounds of the city blaring through my head at all hours of the night and day. I had forgotten what it felt like to be somewhere quiet. Having spent only six months in New York, I sold my furniture, bid my friends farewell, and flew off to Erie.

I thought that if I could find a decent job, maybe life in Erie would be okay. Mom had moved to Austin, Texas; Michael had disappeared and not been heard from for over a year; and Cathy was living in Cincinnati, working again in the mortgage business and seeing her girls during school vacations. I was glad to be back in Erie, but I wouldn't have traded my experience in New York for anything. Journey, "Small Town Girl."

— Chapter Twelve —

It had been twelve long years since I'd left Erie. In the early nineties, with Beej and Mom gone, life there would be a very different experience. I still had a few friends at home. Relatives from my father's side of the family, an aunt and uncle, also lived in the area. Their kids, my cousins, were all grown; some were married with children of their own.

Grandma, who allowed me to stay with her, was none too easy to live with. On a few occasions she'd generously helped me out with money and was now giving me a place to stay. Problem was, while she was often kind and bighearted, other times she was extremely harsh and judgmental. Any help she offered came packaged with an unspoken agreement that entitled her to at least one good future tongue-lashing. Whether I deserved it or not was irrelevant. She liked telling Mom that she'd bought a dress to wear at my wedding, or we could bury her in it—whichever came first. (That dress would fade long before either occurred, much to my silent dismay.)

Sweet little Granny had a mean streak in her that showed itself all too often. When I told her I was going to visit my aunt, she said, "Sure, go run over there. She's had three husbands and you can't even get yourself one." Her disapproval of my lifestyle was always lying in wait. She'd shake her finger at me when I was smoking and say, "A woman who'd do that would do anything." I silently agreed, having no argument with her on that point. She'd have shit her drawers if she'd known a tenth of the truth.

I discovered that my brother Michael had a son, born several years before I moved back to Erie. I was shown pictures of him with my parents and grandma. His mother had once dated Michael. Six years after they broke up, one of Michael's friends told him that he'd seen his ex-girlfriend with a six-year-old boy named Mike who looked just like him. Michael contacted the woman; they reunited and tried to form a relationship, but it didn't work. Afterward, Michael moved to Texas. He was never able to do much for his boy due to his lifestyle. By this time Little Mike was twelve years old. I contacted his mom and went to see him. She acted as both mother and father to Little Mike, and it was easy to see that she loved him very much. I loved getting to know him. He would grow into a fine young man and become another love of my life, along with my nieces.

Shortly after moving back to Erie, I was hired as a sales and marketing representative by a start-up company that built cellular communication sites throughout the country. I was compensated with a generous salary, plus commissions and benefits. I flew first-class all over the country, calling on companies that needed cellular sites. Donnie, the president of the company, trained me, providing me with the information I needed to start making contacts. In the beginning, he accompanied me on calls because of the highly technical nature of the business. Little by little, he hinted at a personal relationship with me, repeating over and over that he could be my special friend. I repeatedly told him that ours was a business relationship and nothing more.

On one of our trips he told me how much he liked to dance, so later at our hotel bar and restaurant when he asked me to dance with him, I did so reluctantly. It was hideous. *He* was hideous. To say that he was unattractive didn't begin to describe him. He sweated profusely and twirled me around with his slimy, sweaty hands. He talked about our being like best friends. I kept repeating that this was strictly business, but he never let up. In between business trips, he often asked me to join him in the conference room for meetings.

One particular day with Diane the office manager in the outer office and his wife using the copy machine, he shut the door to the conference room and talked to me about how he could help me get ready for my soul mate by offering to have sex with me. He said that if I was too uncomfortable to have sex with him in person, we could do it over the phone. *Oh hell no! I know he did not say that!* I thought I'd heard everything; this took the prize for most insane proposition ever. Over the years, this had happened often; it would be easier to list the employers who hadn't propositioned me. My stomach churned and a voice in my head was saying, *What are you doing to me, to us, to this company, after you have invested your life savings along with three other partners? What is the matter with you?* I couldn't believe that this man was saying these things to me with his wife just outside the door.

This had been such a great job, and now it was ruined. By the time I was able to dart out of the conference room, his wife and Diane had left for the day. I left as quickly as I could too. The next day, I called a radio station where I'd interviewed earlier for a sales position. They were still interested and hired me, and I began training in the evenings. They couldn't actually bring me on board until the first of the month, so I kept my job until then. Donnie knew that something was up and asked me to stay after work one day to talk. He said that he didn't want me to leave the company and that I'd misunderstood him the other day. He said that his intentions were to help me, and that it was all perfectly innocent.

I said that if it was all was so innocent, then surely his wife must know all about our conversation. He immediately stopped professing his innocence and offered to lease me a new company car. I accepted his offer on the condition that our relationship would be business only. He agreed. With the car and a good salary, I got my own apartment and moved out of Grandma's house. There was no more trouble from Donnie.

I flew to Dallas for a series of business meetings and stopped to see Mom and Howard in Austin. My stepfather gave me the last known address for Michael. The address was in a dangerous part of Dallas. I knocked on the door, and a little old man in a beard and overalls answered. A strong, unpleasant odor rushed out of the house and assaulted my nostrils. I asked about Michael, stating that I was his sister. The man disappeared behind the door and a heavy-set young woman appeared. She said she thought that Michael was living at the Salvation Army. She told me that Michael was a good man. She was glad to meet me and invited me inside to look up the address in a phone book.

The house was dark and musty. I could barely see or breathe. I noticed some other women and men sitting around the cluttered living room, silently and blankly staring at a television. I was handed the yellow pages and, as I opened the book, huge cock-roaches crawled around everywhere. Some even dropped out of the pages I was thumbing through. It appeared to be raining cock-roaches. The house and furnishings were filthy, cluttered with junk and uneaten food. I wrote down the address and thanked them for their help. I made a quick exit and drove away, crying, imagining Michael warming his hands over a fire over a garbage barrel with other homeless men.

When I arrived at the address, I was surprised to find a large modern building several stories high. I went in and asked for Michael; they told me that it would take a while and to have a seat.

I asked if he lived there and they answered yes. I could hardly believe that I'd found him after all this time. I was so happy that I cried with relief—because I'd found him. My brother eventually came walking down a wide, long staircase. We both smiled huge smiles and were so glad to see each other.

When I told him where I'd been, Michael said that the other place was a crack house he'd stayed in for a time, and that I shouldn't have been there because it was a dangerous place. Over dinner, he told me that he'd been in jail for about a year and had been too ashamed to contact us, even after his release several months before. His car was long gone, and he had very little money. I spent as much time as I could with him over the next week, usually taking him to out to dinner and visiting. It was obvious to me that Michael's drug use had escalated, and he was falling deeper and deeper into the abyss of despair that his life had become.

I contacted Jeanette, the counselor in Dallas, and asked her to help Michael. She agreed to do a trade for yardwork with him. She said that he needed to come to her, explaining that the individual needing help had to make an investment in the process and show a desire to get help. Over dinner, I told Michael about Jeanette. He said that he couldn't afford counseling. I told him about the trade. I asked him if he knew that there was a way for him to be happy and have all the things he wanted, would he want it? He said not to tell our mom, but all he was interested in was getting high. This statement broke my heart. I felt helpless and sorry for him. I told him I loved him. It was hard to leave him, but eventually I had to return to Erie. He was all alone in Dallas, without any family, and not allowed to leave Texas because of probation restrictions. I told him I'd keep in touch and asked him to please call me collect whenever he wanted.

Back in Erie life went on. As a young teenager, I'd made regular visits to a local gynecologist who was known for prescribing birth control pills to adolescents, no questions asked. I started dating Hal, a man I met at a picnic; I returned for a visit to the same doctor. During the gynecological exam there was not a nurse in attendance or anyone else present in the room. While the doctor was performing an internal exam, I felt his finger touch my clitoris and begin to massage it. My head shot up from the table and I gave the doctor a shocked look. He stopped immediately and completed the exam. No words were ever exchanged, but we both knew exactly what he'd done. I did not report him, because to do so didn't even occur to me.

I was just beginning to heal from the rape so many years before, and my reaction was to pretend it didn't happen. There'd been rumors regarding this doctor having sex with patients, which I hadn't believed to be true. However, that was my final visit to him. I realized that those types of predators instinctively know who will remain silent. This latest incident left me feeling too ashamed and guilty to say anything to anyone. This is the first time I have even acknowledged it to anyone.

I'd been seeing Hal for a while when I realized he wasn't very interested in sex. Our sex life was not great to start with and diminished from there. Hal claimed that sex wasn't all it was cracked up to be and was not inclined to do anything to improve the quality of that part of the relationship. In the beginning, we spent an abundance of time talking and getting to know one another. That intimacy disappeared when we were no longer spending one-on-one time together. Hal always made plans for us to do things with other people. I made Hal aware of what I saw happening and asked him to help me regain that feeling of intimacy. He would not. After a year of seeing each other, the relationship had run its course.

I took out all my photograph albums and looked through the many pictures, which were a chronicle of my life. It struck me how, other than the few family photos, most of them were of my friends and me, drunk. A Dallas friend passed out cold in some bathtub; Sally and I perched atop huge chopper bikes in front of Ratskellers, drinking shots; and many, many more. We were always laughing and smiling, with our eyes glazed over. The fun always disappeared the next morning into the loneliness of a painful hangover. Temporary, empty fun. I removed the family photos and threw the albums in the trash. What had happened to all the men I couldn't live without? Why was I still alive if that were really true? What was the point of living anyhow?

Feeling that way, it was no wonder that when I ran into Slick the cop I allowed him to come over to see me a couple of times out of sheer loneliness. I can't explain how I possibly could have allowed him back into my life, but I did and we had sex. The whole thing felt sick and twisted. It was difficult for him to get an erection, which had never been a problem before—I think he probably preferred younger women. That was a fortunate thing for me. I wouldn't have to worry about him pursuing me anymore. At the age of thirty-three I was too old for him. I was relieved, but was left feeling sad and lonely.

Seeing him again brought back many memories, and I began reflecting on our past relationship. I asked Slick if he realized that he'd taken advantage of me at the age of sixteen and that what he'd done was wrong. His response to me was that not only had he not done anything wrong; he'd risked his marriage in order to have a relationship with me. This statement enraged me to the point that I wanted to tear the stuffing out of him, piece by piece. That feeling of rage stayed with me for many years before I was finally able to forgive him.

My old friend Sally and I had stayed in touch. She had moved back to Erie, had remarried, and had two more boys, along with a son from her first marriage. She lived in a nice house and seemed to be doing all right. Her husband, Ralph, had a small take-out restaurant, and she was a clerical worker at a machine shop. They went out every weekend, closing down the bars, and I started going out with them. We had a few more crazy times. Sally and I were a bad combination when it came to drinking—neither of us knew when to stop. Dancing on bars, drinking beer straight out of the tap, and whatever else we could think of. Ralph barely tolerated me being around so much of the time. While we were in a bar one night, Ralph, a weight lifter who liked to show off, grabbed Sally and me by our ankles, lifting us up in the air so that we were hanging upside down. Here we were in the middle of this loud drunken crowd, hanging upside down with our hair dragging in the filthy, beer-soaked and cigarette-butt-littered floor. Tommy James and The Shondells' "Mony Mony" blared from the jukebox.

Living on unemployment compensation, I moved to a less expensive apartment while looking for new work. Diane, the office manager from my last job, and I occasionally hit the bars. One night we stopped by Ratskeller's, one of the dive bars that I'd been going to since I was underage. After a couple of drinks, I climbed on top of the bar in my tight jeans and red sweater and started dancing to the live band because I liked the song they were playing. Diane shouted above the crowd, "No, no, Linda get down from there!" But the crowd loved it, yelling and clapping, cheering me on. Then the lead guitar player had some people carry him over and set him down on the bar next to me as he continued playing. It was great fun; nothing was ever too crazy for me. Over the years I danced on more than a few bars and tabletops in more than a few cities. I always found the willingness to risk making a fool of one's self a highly admirable trait, one that I rarely found in others. My life as a jackass was testimony that I walked my talk, and few would say that.

I began dating a man who worked with Sally. His name was Paul, and he was about eight years younger than I. Paul was a good man, physically fit, and nice-looking too. He had been born in Erie and had lived there his entire life. He worked at a machine shop as a machinist and owned a flat on the east side of town, renting out the first floor and living on the second. He was slowly remodeling the flat in which he lived. The first summer we dated, I went to sixty-plus softball games in which he played. If he wasn't playing sports, he was watching them on television.

We'd been dating a few months when my lease was due to expire. I was looking for an inexpensive apartment and he suggested that I move in with him until I could find one. No one had ever offered to help me out like that; I was touched. I was falling in love with him, and my revived drinking and carousing faded away again. We got along so well that we ended up living together for about a year. I found a part-time day job at a bar near our place where I worked until I found a full-time outside sales job at a beer manufacturer. It was a very low paying position—no car and no benefits.

Our customers were the local bars and restaurants. The first week, one of the reps took me around to train me. We stopped at a place where Sally and I had recently danced on the bar and I'd fallen asleep on top of the pinball machine. The owner mentioned that I looked familiar, but he couldn't place me. I was a bit mortified. I did surprisingly well at that job, considering that I hated it and was paid so little. I opened some new accounts and increased sales in established accounts.

Paul had a bunch of friends and was very well liked. Sometimes I'd look forward to being alone with just him on a Saturday night and staying home to watch a movie together. But there was always some sporting event where the two teams hadn't played each other for fifty thousand years, or something like that, so we often wound up in different rooms, watching different televisions.

I bought a book on relationships and asked Paul to read it. Like many men, he didn't like reading that kind of material so I offered to read it out loud to him, one chapter at a time. He said I was trying to brainwash him. I told him that I wanted to have a better relationship with him. I told him I didn't know how to do that, but I was willing to learn. Perhaps we could learn together. He said no, he wouldn't read the book with me, or have it read to him either. He said that maybe he was already an expert on relationships and didn't need help. I asked him what his dreams were. He said he didn't have any beyond working and fixing his house up. I think he did have dreams. He just was too reserved to share them with me.

During the summer we enjoyed sitting on the front balcony of our second-story apartment, barbequing, eating, and drinking a few beers or glasses of wine and passing food and beers over to our next-door neighbors by way of a bucket on a rope that passed between our two buildings.

Paul and I had joined a bowling team, and on the last night of the season I had a complete meltdown as we prepared to leave the house. I hated my job and our relationship was in a rut. I told him that I wanted to do more with my life. He told me I was too materialistic. I told him it was about more than the money—I wanted to do something I actually enjoyed and had meaning to me. And why shouldn't I be paid more? What was wrong with making lots of money? I was depressed that I couldn't go bowling with him, and he was sad too. I was left feeling guilty for letting him down. He really was a good guy. Why couldn't I just be happy with what I had? I had no answer, only a deep indefinable yearning that left me feeling empty and alone. So utterly alone.

Carolyn, a friend of mine, started talking about moving to Charlotte, North Carolina. She'd researched it and may have even visited there. She asked if I wanted to move there too, explaining that the economy and job market were thriving. I'd loved living in Charlotte as a child and it was always sunny there, which was very appealing after living through a few more of the harsh Erie winters.

I asked Paul to come with me, but he didn't want to leave his longtime job and the flat that he owned. I understood. We were both sad. It was hard to leave him behind, but I knew in the long run it would be the best thing for both of us. I really didn't want to wind up living in Erie permanently. I couldn't pass up the chance to move away again. What I really wanted to do was move to Southern California, but I was too afraid to go there alone. I thought it was too expensive and that I'd never survive there. Charlotte was better than Erie and more affordable than California. Maybe, like in California, the sun would shine there all the time.

CHAPTER THIRTEEN

Living in Charlotte, North Carolina, as a child had been a rare happy time in my life, and I was determined the second time around would be even better. I moved into an apartment with my friend Carolyn temporarily, until her boyfriend moved down from Erie. She quickly found employment, but I had to do a lot of looking. Finally, I applied at a car dealership for a sales position and became the only woman on a sales staff of fifteen. I was not used to retail sales, as all my previous experience had been business to business. This was a very different, challenging environment.

I completed their training program and, by the end of my first month, I'd sold ten cars. This was quite an accomplishment given that I had no previous experience and was brand new in town besides. At first the other guys had been really nice to me, but when they saw how many cars I sold that first month, things quickly turned ugly. One young salesman in particular was very upset that I had done better than he, and he went out of his way to make my life miserable. A couple of his cohorts joined him in his little pranks—like letting the air out of my tires—but he was the ringleader. One day, he told me to my face I had no right to be in that business because I was a woman. He was angry and dead serious, but no matter what they did or how they tried to slip me up, I tried to stay focused on doing my job. It didn't help when a prospect ran over a cat on a test drive, much to my horror, and the sales manager was only concerned about the car.

I met quite a few people and my social life was going well. I received a constant flow of invitations to various events. I'd always enjoyed decorating, cooking, baking, cleaning, and the domestic life, so I began hosting mimosa brunches and throwing cocktail or margarita parties for my new group of friends. Because of my wild side and some of the things I soon became known for—like my "Topless Service Upon Request," which was stenciled on the kitchen wall above my stove—they called me "the X-rated Martha Stewart."

Though my social life was in full swing, the harassment at the car dealership never subsided. After nearly a year of working sixty to seventy hours a week, all of them drama-filled, I quit. It was just too difficult. Through a lead from Carolyn, I interviewed with an industrial plating company for an outside sales position. Two men, both named Daniel, owned the company. Both interviewed me, but Tall Daniel spent more time with me. I quickly realized that he ran the show. I could also tell that he liked my long legs as I crossed them and he admired them throughout our meeting. I kidded myself that I wasn't playing with fire and was soon hired at a very comfortable salary, plus commissions, benefits, and, in three months, the promise of a company car.

I had no personal interest in Tall Daniel, only the job and the compensation. My new boss had just been through a bitter divorce. Evidently, he'd been caught cheating and was kicked out of his home. He saw nothing wrong with cheating and hated his wife for divorcing him. Most people have an adjustment period after divorce before returning to the dating world, but not TD, because he'd never stopped dating. Though he was currently involved with a woman who worked in the shop, right away he started with the sexual remarks to me. I needed the job too much to say anything. I just let it go in one ear and out the other.

I started making appointments and calling on potential accounts, to which TD or D often accompanied me. Typically, we had to drive a couple of hours to see a prospective client. I brought a fair amount of new business to the company. However, the two Ds were not very good businessmen and even worse managers. They'd bought the company from the widow of the man who used to own it. Their philosophy was that they didn't like how their former employers had treated them, so now that they owned their own company, they were working to create a place where people would be treated well. It was a bunch of hogwash.

As fast as I brought new accounts in one door, established accounts flew out the other. Plating is a very precise science, and there were problems in quality control. TD's answer was more sales. To make matters worse, a woman had just left after embezzling money from the company right under the two Ds' noses. They didn't talk about it, but the women who ran the office told me. Behind his girlfriend's back, TD asked me for a date. I told him no way, under no circumstances; I just wanted to work there and do a good job. I was grateful when he stopped pursuing me. If things kept on this way, I was going to be out of a job again. It was not a good situation.

Then the fun really began. TD gave me the silent treatment, or worse, abused me in all kinds of petty ways. He went through my notes when I was not there and called my customers, asking questions. He assigned me tasks and asked for my conclusions, and, based on research, I gave him knowledgeable answers. He told me that he didn't want to do what I'd suggested, and I politely responded that as the owner of the company he could do whatever he wanted. He became angry with me and told me he didn't hire me to be a "yes man." It was crazy-making.

I talked to D about the situation, but when they were handing out balls, he thought they said dolls, and passed. D would not confront TD even though he could see the problems. It was miserable. My job became a living hell I was trapped in every day. Though I knew he was a hound from the first minute I'd met him, when his eyes wandered everywhere except to my face. I knew I'd encouraged him because I was desperate for a job and an income. I had rent and bills to pay, and couldn't afford to quit.

I knew I had to change our relationship. I'd decided that being "right" had gotten me nowhere. I dropped my anger and my need to be right. I said to TD, "Look, whatever happened between us, I am sorry. You can blame everything on me. I don't care. I just want to work here and enjoy it if that is possible. Is there any way that you can forgive me and we could make a fresh start?" TD finally softened, because I meant every word and he knew it. We made peace and I was finally given my company car.

I'd made some friends at the car dealership who lived on a lake about thirty miles north of Charlotte. I began hanging out, boating, and partying with them. This group of people were all heavy drinkers, and it wasn't long before I'd slipped back into the drinking scene. Everyone was part of a couple and I often felt lonely. I occasionally bumped into Craig, a man I had known for a couple of years. I had always been attracted to him but hadn't said anything because he was married. It had been a long time since I'd dated a married man; it was the last thing I ever thought I'd do again. My little voice was speaking wisdom to me, but, as usual, I managed to ignore it.

I was used to being the one who was pursued, not the other way around. I always attracted men very easily, but rarely anyone I felt attracted to. Besides, the men I usually attracted were as broken as I was, in one way or the other. My girlfriends loved going out with me because they always met men when they were with me. Then I wouldn't hear from them until they were "single" again.

In an unusual move, I called and suggestively invited Craig over, but he said he couldn't make it. Then he showed up at my door. I'd known and admired him for a couple of years; he was no stranger to me. He'd never made a flirtatious move toward me, and I didn't think this was something he'd done before. Craig was a few years older than I, intelligent (except at that particular moment), handsome, and a sharp dresser. He always smelled good, had a great physique, and was very sexy to me. Possibly the sexiest man I'd ever known. I found all that southern gentleman, daarrrlin' gimme sum shuga talk in a sexy southern drawl simply irresistible. He was mostly bald, but it didn't matter; some men can pull it off. I told him he was too sexy for his hair. I had on an emerald green silk slip with spaghetti straps. We sat and talked for a while on the couch and had a couple of drinks. Our initial nervousness melted away with the alcohol and was replaced by burning desire.

It was hard to ignore that there was only a thin layer of silk between my nakedness and us. When he touched my arm I felt his heat. Pounding hearts, racing pulses. I was on him like white on rice. We made love and it set me on fire. Lips, breasts, bodies, soft, wet, hard, two become one. I was crazy with wanting him after that. It was totally mutual. Marvin Gaye, "Let's Get It On" . . . oh yeah.

He told me right from the start that he'd never leave his wife. He was always in such a hurry when he came over, and I always tried in vain to make him slow down. I was about forty and at my sexual peak. (I might possibly be having my sexual peak all over again just from writing this!) Our affair lasted for a few months, nearly a year, but when the holidays rolled around, I decided to break it off. I couldn't deal with it. I loved him and wanted to be with him, and I knew that would never happen. Craig was my last married man. The needle scratches across the record, ending in a thump, then . . . silence. "Gettin' it on" . . . over baby.

I was laid off from my job with TD when they could no longer afford to pay me. I worked briefly for another company as a sales representative before I finally decided to exit the corporate world for good. I was forty years old, and I'd worked my entire adult life doing things I didn't want to do. I gave away thousands of dollars' worth of clothing to a friend and promised myself that I'd never wear that type of clothing again. I threw my resume in the trashcan too. Then I asked myself, *What am I good at and what do I love doing?* I came up with organizing; I'd come out of Mom's womb folding my own diapers. I'd been organizing my whole life. No one had ever taught me how to do it; I was just instinctively good at it. I didn't know if anyone would actually pay me to do it, but I was determined to spend my days doing what I loved.

On my fortieth birthday, a group of friends celebrated with me at an elegant restaurant over delicious food and enough champagne to take a bath in. I danced on the table with a man who'd fought in two world wars before I was born. I was overweight, drinking heavily, still wearing the occasional lampshade on the head, eating ice cream, cake, cheese, and deep-fried everything. I smoked over three packs of menthol cigarettes a day and was deep in debt—again. The broken record of my life was playing *broke and fucked up, broke and fucked up, broke and fucked up.* Hey, I never said my life was a Hallmark greeting card. Dysfunction . . . was my main function.

I used the commission money from my last sales job to move to Cornelius, just north of Charlotte. I rented a beautiful two-bedroom, two-bathroom apartment with a wood-burning fireplace right on Lake Norman and a stone's throw from a marina, a restaurant, and a bar. I decorated my new apartment lovingly, making it even more beautiful. I thought that if I only did work that I loved doing, had a nice place to live, and had a nice car, that I'd have a good life— even without a romantic partner. I thought that somehow I'd be okay and everything would work out. Otis Redding, "(Sittin' On) The Dock of the Bay." The only problem was . . . everything.

The combination of my drinking and inner turmoil caused me to behave erratically at times. One day I was happy and friendly, and the next I'd be harsh and judgmental. Or sometimes I'd be on top of my game and everything would run smoothly, then I'd wake up the next day and it seemed that everything was falling apart in Linda Land. This, plus my heavy drinking, alienated many of my friends. The few that I had left were just as crazy and mixed up as I was. Sometimes when I went out I got so drunk I couldn't stand up. Other times I'd get so drunk I'd just disappear without telling anyone, and they worried about me. I was told that I sometimes used foul language, which I did not recall. I had some blackouts, with no memory of what had taken place for hours at a time. The hangovers I suffered on the mornings after were excruciating. I despised hangovers, and they became a huge motivator for me to stop drinking. I was tired of my crazy, mixed-up life.

I made and distributed flyers, and people started hiring me to organize their lives. Many of the houses on Lake Norman were huge multimillion-dollar mansions. The manager of the local yacht club invited me to give a workshop one night. About fifteen people attended, mostly women, some of whom hired me. I started getting steady jobs for which I was paid quite well. I'd worked for so many years of my life performing jobs I didn't enjoy. Now I worked harder than ever before for the opportunity to do work that I loved. My clients were pleased with my organizing abilities, and word spread. Still, there were times I had plenty of work, other times when I had none. Running my own business was a struggle financially.

I was invited to a party on the lake, where I met a man named Devlin. He was older than me but looked good for his age. He was tall, dark, cute—and a total dickweed. He had an extremely deep, sexy voice and lived next door to the hosts in a trailer. I heard he threw some pretty wild parties in the summer. It was just the beginning of spring and still a little cold. We drank, smoked hash, and danced all night. I, along with several others, was invited to spend the night since we were in no condition to drive. Devlin invited me next door to his place, saying he had plenty of room. I passed out in the bed while he slept out on the couch.

When I woke up in the morning, Devlin showed me around his place. He'd built a huge deck on the lakeshore, complete with a kitchen, bar, and upstairs sun deck, and was finishing a fabulous bathroom and shower house. There were beautiful hanging plants everywhere and a huge vegetable garden in another part of the yard. He lived in a little old dinky travel trailer with this huge, elaborate deck—you could have lived on the deck except there were no walls. He drove me back to my car at the neighbor's house, and I drove off hung-over as all hell.

The little voice said, *For the love of God, no, not him, I beg of you.*

Of course, for the next year-and-a-half, we had on-again/off-again, butt-spanking, wild, crazy sex. He saw me in between hosting his parties on the deck and only really pursued me outside of the summer party season. Devlin knew exactly what to say, while he didn't mean a word. He had no conscience whatsoever. He was completely charming, making me feel like a queen one day, then tossing me aside like yesterday's trash. Through the grapevine, I heard that he was bisexual and a swinger. Women weren't his first choice, but being with a man was something he felt had to be hidden. He was also a serious alcoholic, drinking from the time he woke up until he went to bed at night. Other than these minor issues, he would have made a fine knight in shining armor.

At one point, Devlin convinced me to make an appointment with a plastic surgeon to consider having my breasts augmented. I agreed to the consultation, thinking that just maybe larger breasts might buoy me up out of the sea of shit my life had become. That brilliant idea fell by the wayside when I couldn't afford the steep price tag. Shortly afterward, our relationship finally came to a permanent end. My main clients divorced and my income dwindled, leaving me hanging by a thread again. I began to turn toward spiritual teachings more and more, looking for answers. Drinking and spending myself into oblivion was running its course. There had to be a better way.

In addition to the teachings of Shirley MacLaine, Maya Angelou, and Marianne Williamson, I was drawn to others like Louise Hay, Dan Millman, Richard Bach, Dr. Wayne Dyer, Deepak Chopra, Gary Zukav, Don Miguel Ruiz, Eckhart Tolle, Dr. Brad Blanton, and others. All of these teachers helped further my spiritual journey. Then, on Thanksgiving Day at my sister Cathy's house, someone placed a book in my hands that opened my mind even more and helped me take even more steps up the ladder of my spiritual awakening.

The book was *Conversations with God, Book 1,* by Neale Donald Walsch. I eventually read and it loved it; it asked and answered some of the big questions I was asking. I listened to that first book and his follow-up works, *CwG, Book 2, CwG, Book 3, Friendship with God,* and *Communion with God,* on cassette tape as soon as they were published. For the next four years I listened to them over and over again from beginning to end, nearly every day of my life. His pronouncement that anyone who smoked cigarettes or consumed alcohol showed very little will to live was a cold, hard slap in my face. I knew it was true, and the realization throbbed gently in my consciousness from that moment on. I opened my mind to many higher truths. Mr. Walsch taught me that we are all one, I am truly that which needs nothing, life is eternal, God is perfect love, the world is an illusion, all conflict is within, and so much more. As my mind started to change, so did my life.

Bella, my beautiful, dark-haired, five-feet-three-inch fireball friend, visited me late one summer night. She was admittedly lousy at navigating her own ship, but quite good at telling everybody else exactly where they were fucking up with deadly accuracy. As Bella and I drank and smoked up a storm as usual, on this particular evening she had the audacity to tell me that I did not walk my talk.

I didn't know it, but she'd had sex with Devlin at a time I was not seeing him and was all too aware of every detail of Devlin's sexual proclivities. She was upset with me for falling on my face and gave me a good bitching out, saying that I was the one she and our other friends looked up to. I was supposed to know better and be the one to set a good example. This pissed me off, and we had a heated argument with many insults being hurled back and forth. Eventually, I was forced to throw her ass out the door. After she left, I realized that she was right. I didn't have the answers, but I was determined to find them.

I stayed up all night, thinking and smoking and thinking some more. I was nearly out of cigarettes. There was a store open twenty-four hours if I wanted more, but something inside of me said, "No." By sunrise I'd smoked my last cigarette. I heard a voice within me say, *That is the last cigarette you'll ever smoke for the rest of your life.* I called Mom and told her I'd quit smoking, and that I'd never smoke again for the rest of my life. When I told her that I'd just quit that morning, she burst out laughing. I had to laugh too—I'd smoked for thirty years, three or more packs a day. I cleared all the alcohol out of my apartment, because I couldn't imagine drinking without smoking. Slowly but surely, I was gaining my will to live.

I never took so much as a puff on another cigarette, or struggled with that addiction ever again. I hadn't even tried to quit, because I liked smoking even though it was disgusting. The addiction just fell off of me like a leaf falls off of a tree—that's how easy it was. It was truly a miracle.

For so many years my invisible broken, jagged edges had acted like magnets to the invisible broken, jagged edges of other damaged souls. Something momentous was happening. I was beginning to collect myself and pick up the pieces of my shattered self. Perhaps there'd come a time when I'd become whole within myself and no longer able to mesh with another's broken, jagged edges, as my own edges would become healed and smoothed over until they disappeared altogether.

— CHAPTER FOURTEEN —

I wanted to do something more with my life, other than the organizing. I felt drawn to write, but had no confidence in my ability. I wrote all the time, but always threw my work away. I loved to read, and every time I finished a book, I asked myself how could I do better than that, and why did the world need a book from me? One day I heard a loud clear voice within my head say, *It is not about being better, it is about being different.* I knew then I'd some-day write a book.

It had been a struggle since I left the corporate world not hav-ing a regular paycheck, always playing catch-up to pay my bills and promising my creditors that they'd receive payment soon. I made the difficult decision to file bankruptcy for the second time in my life. William, the man who'd previously hired me at the car rental company, located me somehow. He was working for a different car rental company based in Atlanta, Georgia, and he told me that a marketing representative position was open in Clearwater, Florida. It had been a while since I'd received a regular paycheck and I thought that it would be nice to not live in a constant state of worry over where my next buck was coming from. I also wanted to be near the ocean and endless summers. I sold or gave away my belongings, said my farewells, packed my car, and headed for Florida.

It was a tremendous amount of work to continually be on the run but that didn't stop me.

The job turned out to be a poor choice. It paid me barely enough to live on, and the company was not doing well operationally or financially. After losing my last car to bankruptcy, I bought a five-year-old Mercury Cougar for ten thousand dollars with a loan, which had a ridiculously high interest rate due to my atrocious credit score. I probably paid for that car two or three times over. Aside from the interest rate and the ninety-year-old drunken salesman who tried to make a date (code for a hand job), which I politely turned down, getting the car was a fairly easy process. I drove to my place, packed up my new car, and headed back to North Carolina, only six months after I had left. My life was changing, but I still seemed to be constantly on the move.

I stayed with a former neighbor and friend named Mick until I could find my own place. I had been drug, alcohol, and tobacco free for almost a year. During that year I'd gained some weight, but through healthier eating and exercise it was coming off. Since quitting smoking I was drawn to hike and walk more and more. I was almost forty-three years old, and my twenty-fifth high school reunion was just around the corner. I wasn't sure whether or not I should go. Then my grandmother, my mother's mother, died the week before the reunion.

I drove to Erie for the funeral. Cathy came from Ohio, but our brother Michael didn't make it. After the funeral Cathy went home and I attended my twenty-fifth. This was my first sober reunion, so I volunteered to be the designated driver for some of my classmates. I called an old friend, Beverly, who was also still single, and asked her to be my "date" for the weekend. The reunion lasted two nights; we went to dinner with several other classmates before the first night's event. Then we headed over to the place where all our other classmates were gathering.

I made the rounds and visited with as many people as I could. Kevin was there. We talked and caught up on what was happening in each other's lives. He was married and had children. We pretended to talk easily, as if we had no past. I didn't want there to be any ill feelings between us, but didn't know how to fix it. I just wanted to be able to go to my reunion and feel normal and good about myself without feeling knee-deep in the past. To end the first night, we all headed over to a local bar.

The next night I went to the dinner dance with Beverly. We ate, visited, and danced. I saw Kevin again, and he introduced me to his wife. I could tell he had something on his mind; he seemed apprehensive. Later he came over and said privately, "We need to talk." The two of us met at a restaurant for breakfast the following morning. Kevin told me that during high school he'd noticed me and had wanted to talk to me, but had never been able to bring himself to approach me. He apologized for raping me. He said that he wanted to start a friendship with me. I agreed that we could start building a friendship, because I felt he was being sincere. All the questions I had surrounding the rape began to surface. I began asking them as a part of the healing. I asked him if he'd ever had counseling regarding the rape. He told me he hadn't and that he'd never discussed it with anyone. I asked if he knew the others involved; he said he knew one of them but couldn't recall exactly how many were involved.

Upon returning to North Carolina, I contacted my old organizing clients and was able to get some work and generate some much-needed income. Mick had just bought a condominium and would be moving shortly. I asked him if I could stay at his condo for a while in exchange for packing, unpacking, and organizing his new home. He agreed. We moved into the new place, and he was very happy with how nicely I arranged his new home. I had him settled in within a couple of days.

Mick owned a boat, and he took me out on it with his children a few times. On my forty-third birthday, he took me out to dinner. I mentioned that I had a date in a few days with someone whom I'd recently met. He became visibly upset but said nothing. When we got home he went into his room and closed his door; he refused to speak to me for several days. When I went out on my date Mick was not home, and he was in bed when I returned. A few days later, Mick apologized for acting that way. He explained that had feelings for me and hoped that we'd become a couple. I told him that while I didn't have romantic feelings for him, I appreciated everything he'd done for me. I made sure to let him know that I'd be leaving soon.

I moved into a plush one-bedroom apartment in a fairly new complex with all the amenities. I had my own brand-new washer and dryer and a large sunken bathtub. The first night I was in my new place, I was awakened by loud knocks on the door at about two in the morning. I could see a couple of huge thug-looking guys through the peephole. They said they had an order to repossess my car. I opened the door and told them it was a mistake. I'm sure they'd heard that one before, but this time it was true. I'd moved back to North Carolina from Florida immediately after purchasing my car. That, coupled with my poor credit rating, caused the automobile finance company to cancel the loan. I found this out when I had contacted them with my new address. A few phone calls later, I was assured by the dealership that another loan from a different source would be made.

I thought matters had been straightened out, but here these thugs were trying to grab my car. I asked them how they found me. They said Mick told them the name of the apartment complex and they had been going door to door, knocking and making a commotion, looking for me. The thugs asked for my keys. I brought my keys with me and went out to the car. As I was collecting my belongings, preparing to relinquish my car to them, a police cruiser pulled up to answer a call from one of my new neighbors. The officer asked to see the thugs' papers. He told them that they did not have the proper paperwork and me that I was not required to surrender my car.

While the thugs and the policeman were talking, I drove to a phone booth and called Mick. I told him that I couldn't believe he'd told two strange and dangerous-looking men my address—in the middle of night no less. He said he thought they were friends of mine and that he'd been out of it because he'd been awakened from a sound sleep. I didn't believe him, but I kept quiet. Mick met me and together we parked my car in a place where they'd never find it. The next day, I was informed that an additional eight hundred dollars was needed to finance a new loan. I didn't have the extra money since I'd just paid rent and a security deposit. Mom called me because the repo people had contacted her. She asked if she could help, and somehow she worked it out and sent the money to me. I was able to get the loan and reclaim the use of my car.

I was so shaken by these events that I once again seriously considered suicide as a solution. I was so tired of the ongoing battle that was my life. But receiving that money from Mom gave me hope that I could make a new life for myself. I continued to work organizing people's homes, but it was a struggle to pay the rent on time each month.

I went out on a few more dates with Doug, the man I'd first seen while I lived at Mick's. He had two young children and an ex-wife who'd cheated on him and then divorced him. He didn't bother to hide his bitterness and anger toward her, and was very closed off emotionally. His main appeal was his financial stability, which he'd established through his own custom-home construction business. He was just my type of unhappiness—by now we all know what the little voice was saying! I thought that if I settled for someone with financial security, life wouldn't be so bad. The problem—and the blessing—was that Doug wasn't that into me. We didn't have sex until we'd known each other for a while, and I allowed it to happen, hoping that maybe it would bond us somehow.

I was still prostituting myself, like I had my whole life. Whether I was directly selling my body for sexual acts, working at a job I hated in order to survive, having sex to be loved and/or taken care of, or doing anything my heart was not into, they were all some form of prostitution. Repeatedly doing what I thought I had to do in order to survive in this world instead of being true to myself was an inner war I fought every day. My outer circumstances were merely a reflection of my inward condition, all of which seemed to be out of my control. The inner darkness that lived within me made me a derelict to self-honor.

I continued to have disturbing nightmares, but they occurred less and less often. Sometimes I tried to make myself wake up in the middle of them. Always I woke up scared and sweaty. I would fall back to sleep, still scared. In the morning light, I was relieved that the darkness of the night was gone and on the surface I felt a little safer.

True to his word, Kevin stayed in touch with me, working on building some kind of a friendship. We communicated by phone and sometimes by email. He wanted to meet me at a restaurant halfway between our cities to have breakfast, which was a several-hour drive. I agreed to meet him, but when the appointed day arrived I didn't want to go. Instead of canceling, I slept in, making for a late start. To make matters worse, I got lost. Kevin was at the restaurant waiting for me when I finally arrived and questioned me about what had delayed me. I told him I had gotten lost on the way.

We sat down to eat, and he continued questioning me. I heard myself defending myself to him! He abruptly announced that he didn't know what he was doing there. I asked him if his wife knew about our meeting, and he said no. That made me feel very uncomfortable, like he was trying to start something with me. I was beginning to get the idea that he wanted to have sex with me, as if that would somehow cancel out the past.

Kevin became confrontational. He told me that he'd planned to be able to spend more time with me, but because I was hours late he wouldn't be able to. He was clearly upset. Finally, we talked about the rape. He told me he didn't know why he did it, but that after he raped me, he'd felt a tremendous release. After the release, he felt confused. When I heard that I felt sick to my stomach. I had to get out of there, get in my car and drive home. I told him I had to go, escaped into my car, and drove off. I was very relieved to be away from him.

A few days later, I called Kevin. I told him that I didn't hate him, but I couldn't continue this "friend" thing. I urged him to get some counseling. I told him that I was doing my best to deal with the rape but was in no position to help him—it was his responsibility to resolve his own issues. We did not speak again.

My relationship with Doug never solidified; after several attempts, it ended just a few days shy of my forty-fourth birthday. He told me that he was just a steppingstone in my life on the way to greater things. I cried because I was so tired of struggling. All I wanted was to be able to spend my days doing what I loved doing, have enough money to live comfortably, and have someone to share my life with. I got down on my knees and cried out to God that if there was a way to have heaven on Earth, then he had better show me, because I was not willing to live a mediocre life, going from one dead-end relationship to the next and either working at jobs I hated in order to pay the rent, or doing work I loved while unable to take care of myself. I was dead serious. I would rather be dead than live my life as I had been. I couldn't go on as I had.

That night I went to bed and fell asleep. I woke up, but my body still lay asleep. I was in an awakened dream "experience." I had never known anything like it before or since. There are no words to adequately describe it, but I was one with everything. I was not out of my body, because I had no body. I was not a body. I saw and heard, but not with human eyes and ears. It was like floating in an endless, dark blue space with swirling masses of stars, mixed with many points of light, sprinkled across space. I heard a voice speaking to me. I thought it was God's voice. The voice guided me to observe how it felt. It felt beyond blissful.

Then the voice guided me to turn my attention to the body and the personality of Linda Jean McNabb for observation. For the very first time in my life, I was able to see and appreciate myself. I felt immense love for this brave and loving person who'd been through so much. I was told so many things that I knew I would not recall them when I awoke. I thought for a moment that the voice was my voice. Then I realized there was only one voice in all of true reality.

As soon as I woke up the next morning, I began writing. After a few days, I felt guided to entitle the book *Wisdomism,* a word I had awakened with a couple of years before. After that dream I felt more at peace, like I had an inner knowledge, even though I could not define it. I started seeing an iridescent, indigo-blue flash of light. (To this day it still shows up sporadically.) I could "hear" an inner voice speaking to me, giving me guidance. It told me to leave everything and go west. I said no way! I'd moved too many times; I couldn't start over again and give up the comfort of my home to travel west. I'd started from scratch too many times. The voice said, *Just do it, and when you come out the other side, you will never want for anything ever again. Liquidate and make a pilgrimage to see your family.*

Somehow I was able to trust that inner voice and move forward. It was not an easy thing to do. I didn't even use the word *pilgrimage* in my vocabulary, and yet I was willing to follow the voice and go on one! I said good-bye to my friends and once again sold or gave away most of my things, then packed the rest into my car. Frank Sinatra, "That's Life."

I didn't have a clue how everything would work out, yet I heeded the voice and headed north to my family before the trip west. I was fortunate to be present for the birth of my nephew Mike's baby girl—my brother Michael's first grandchild. While visiting Cathy, I found out that she had some serious legal problems concerning a business she used to own with a woman partner. Cathy was in way over her head and didn't know what to do, other than pray that the worst wouldn't happen. She was in a lot of pain, and I was very worried about her. I know there were times she thought about taking her own life. There was not much I could do to help her. I was still in a lot of pain myself trying to figure out my own life, occasionally drinking again.

I was very hesitant to leave and begin a new life out west. This was the first time I was moving somewhere when guided by my inner voice and not as a means of running away from my life. I was looking forward to seeing Michael for the first time in several years, and that finally got me moving. I'd longed to see him again for years, but had been unable to afford the expense of travel. Finally, I hugged everyone good-bye and hit the road, God help me, *again*. My life had been like a bad country-western song, "Looking for Love in All the Wrong Places." I'd been good and bad and everything in between. I was ready for a new day and a new song.

— PART THREE —

She looked down from the mountaintop
Wanting desperately to leap off,
To spread her wings and fly at last.

Not a care in the world,
Not a worry or plea,
Her soul has been released,
There's not a tear left to shed.

She looks up and sees a light above,
She feels a sense of relief,
Although she is alone, she no longer feels empty.
Free . . . she is finally free

—Sarah M. Montesi

— Chapter Fifteen —

I drove for a couple of days, stopping along the way to sleep, before arriving in Dallas and a much-anticipated reunion with my brother Michael. When I saw him standing on a street corner, I could see the heavy toll years of drug use had taken on his face. I fought back tears as I pulled over to pick him up and felt a rush of crisp cold air hit me in the face as he climbed into the car. I asked him where he wanted to eat; he said it didn't matter. I asked if the Spaghetti Factory was okay, and he said yes. His face wasn't the only thing that had changed. He was not the same. He'd been beaten down by life.

I learned that he was living in a men's shelter and worked construction for minimum wage. He'd spent the previous night in the emergency room waiting to be treated for several spider bites that had become infected. He showed me his hand, which was swollen from the bites. I asked him what happened to his other hand, why it too was all swollen. He said that's how it always was. Of course, I knew why—his hands were permanently swollen from years of fighting. We laughed. I noticed that one of his front teeth next to his four front false teeth was black and rotten with a big hole in it. I wondered how it had all come to this. Seeing my brother this way broke my heart.

In the restaurant he pulled out a pair of glasses to read the menu, the kind you buy for a few dollars at the drugstore that sit low on the bridge of your nose. They were just like ones Beej had worn. We just looked at each other and had an even bigger laugh as he put them on to read the menu and peered out over the top of the lenses at me. Many years had passed since we endured our traumatic childhood, taking our youth for granted.

I told my brother how very much I loved him and that we all loved him no matter what. He said it was true that we'd never given up on him. I knew that our love made a difference in his life. After Beej died, I had realized that the time to tell people how you feel is while they are still alive, although later I would come to learn that those you truly love never leave you.

The night before I headed west, I picked up Michael and treated him to dinner at our favorite restaurant on the side of town where we all used to live. Michael was always able to eat more than anyone I'd ever known, with the exception of Beej, and he politely asked before ordering if it was okay with me. I told him to order whatever he desired. That such a small thing made him happy made my heart fill with love for him. I only wished I could do more. Afterward, we stopped at a store and bought bug killer and some other things he needed. On the way back to the shelter, we stopped at a coffee shop and I bought him a pastry and something to drink. I didn't have much money, but what I had I spent freely on Michael. He was nearing fifty, indigent, and living in a shelter. He had even less than I did, and I was going to do everything I possibly could. I knew I could always manage to get more money, somehow.

I left him with a batch of chocolate chip cookies I'd baked and a little color television with a built-in VCR that I'd packed in my trunk. He was pleased; there was a Clint Eastwood film festival showing that weekend and now he'd be able to watch it. Michael didn't want me to go, and while it was hard for me to leave him I knew that my life was waiting for me somewhere else. I told Michael that I thought I was on my way to California and that I was going there to rebuild my life. I didn't know how I'd do it, but someday when I was able and he was free from parole, I'd bring him out to start a new life. I asked him if he'd like that and he said yes, but I don't think he ever expected it to happen.

I dropped him at the brick men's shelter institution where he lived, with his cookies and little TV that he was so pleased to have. I watched as he struggled to carry it inside, walking through the stark coldness of the lighted gravel parking lot to the guarded entrance. I wasn't allowed to help him. I had to stay outside of the high, chain-link fence and gates. He turned back and smiled at me as we waved good-bye and the guard checked him in for the night. I drove away with tears in my eyes, wishing I could have done more, but I knew in my heart that the best thing I could do for both of us was to figure out my own life. Marvin Gaye, "I Heard It through the Grapevine."

Early the next morning, I was on the road again—on my way to California, or some point in between. I really wasn't sure. I just drove west until I couldn't drive any farther, stopping along the way in a parking lot to sleep one night to conserve what money I had left. I arrived in San Diego late at night. I found a motel and decided to spend one night there so that I could bathe and have a good night's sleep. When I checked out, I was left with about fifty dollars to my name.

The next day I drove to San Clemente and headed for the beach. It was the first week in February, and the Santa Ana winds were blowing, making it as warm as a summer's day. I slipped into my bikini and walked the beach barefoot for six miles. I decided that this was what I was born to do.

I certainly hadn't planned to live in my car—it just happened. I was not scared one bit, except at night, when it was dark. I was afraid that the police would find me and I'd get fined, or that a stranger might see me and try to hurt me. At first, I felt ashamed that I now lived in my car—for about two seconds. Then I realized that this did not define me and that I had a higher purpose in moving there. As far as having no money and no idea how I would survive, I had no fear. I knew it would all work out. Arriving in California was the beginning of a whole new lifestyle for me.

My desire to drink finally left me for good, just as easily and miraculously as my former tobacco addiction. I became extremely conscious of what I was putting in my mouth and on my body. Over the next few months, between walking on the beach every day and eating only healthy food, I lost twenty pounds. I looked and felt better than I ever had. I'd gone from literally years of standing hair and nail appointments, cable television, Oprah-watching, couch potato remote-button-pushing, chocolate martini margarita champagne sipping maniac, bar dancing, sunken tub bubble baths, three hundred and fifty thread count sheets, more appliances and amenities than a third world country, candy bar cheese puff ice cream potato chip meals, to living in my car and a totally new and healthy lifestyle almost overnight. While my acrylic nails grew out, and I was in full-on menopause, I began rebuilding my life from the inside out.

I lived at 1995 Mercury Cougar Lane, and had never felt so free or happy in my life. Southern California was blue skies sunshine clean beach ocean air endless summer. I felt like the luckiest person alive!

∽

After San Clemente, I looked at a map and settled on Encinitas in northern San Diego County as the place to live. After a couple of nights of sleeping in parking lots and laying low, I pulled into a state beach lot. Still wearing my pajamas from the night before, I rummaged through my trunk. I'd noticed there were places that paid cash for clothes, and I needed cash and more room in my car. I was reorganizing my things when a couple of surfers parked nearby to check out the waves. One of them came over and talked to me. I had North Carolina plates and a car full of clothes, pillows, and a blanket. It was probably obvious that I was living in my car, though I didn't advertise that fact. Along with a few other helpful tips, one of the guys told me about a gym where the owner was known to trade work in exchange for a gym membership, which meant access to hot showers. I thanked him for his help and went on my way.

I brought some select pieces of clothing to one of the stores that advertised "cash for clothes" and exchanged them for a few dollars. I donated the clothes I couldn't sell to make more room in my car. Then I went to the gym the surfer had told me about and introduced myself to the owner, Tom. I told him that I was very good at organizing, and if he needed some help, could I trade a gym membership in exchange for my work? I started working that day and was luxuriating in a hot shower by nightfall. When I worked up enough courage to explain to Tom that I was living in my car, he graciously allowed me to park in his lot.

I now had a place to take hot showers, a safe place to park, and a warm car in which to sleep. I was deeply grateful, because every day I saw others who had so much less. I discovered Moonlight Beach, which instantly became my favorite, as I sustained my newly acquired habit of walking on the beach and appreciating every sunset. I started to get to know some of the locals who hung out there. There was Ben, who had lived in his van since his young son had committed suicide a couple years before. One day he just walked over to my car window and handed me a ten-dollar bill for food. I thanked him and knew I'd never forget his kindness and generosity. There was the fisherman, a retired school superintendent, whom I'd spot standing in the water up to his knees, with his bright thick head of white hair sticking out from under his hat and the strong pungent smell of his cigar wafting over to me as he cast his pole into the waters. One day, I introduced myself and found out his life story.

Tom had been looking for someone to organize him, so I happened along at just the right time. He gave me a full year's gym membership and also started paying me by the hour. After the work ran out, so did my money. There were days I only had thirty-four cents to my name, but I felt happy and free, really for the first time in my life. I decided that I would not have any material possessions unless they came to me easily and without effort. I didn't wish to buy things on credit or owe money to people anymore.

I'd meditated a little when I lived in North Carolina, but never regularly. Now, in the west, I was immediately drawn to meditate once or twice a day. I found a huge pile of rocks near the bluffs about a mile north of Moonlight Beach. I perched myself on those rocks and meditated. Jesus would come and invite me to join him in a big crystal castle in the sky. A colossal white Pegasus would appear on the beach. In my mind's eye, I would climb atop the Pegasus with Jesus and we would fly away to the castle. There was a round room on the top floor of the castle, with open windows all the way around and a fire pit in the middle.

Jesus and I would sit facing each other, with our legs folded in front of us as we talked. He'd ask me what I'd like my life to be and we'd discuss it. Sometimes I'd sit on his lap, or sometimes I'd lay my head in his lap as he stroked my hair, speaking gentle words or saying nothing at all. Sometimes he'd be the one to sit in my lap or lay his head there. Other times, we'd stand up and dance around the room. He became my best friend whom I visited every day and every night. My nightmares and depression faded away, and thoughts of suicide came less and less often.

One day a newspaper was placed into my hands. I intuitively circled an ad for a caregiver position of an elderly woman with Alzheimer's. The next day, I walked on the beach, showered, and changed. I was permitted to use a phone at the gym, so I called and spoke to the daughter of the woman who needed help. I made an appointment with her and knew the job would be mine if I wanted it. I had three years of payments left on my car and the bill was about ninety days past due. I'd called the finance company and told them where I was. I kept calling, promising that I'd pay soon.

At the interview I met Marge and her mother Dolly, whom I'd care for in their nice private home nearby. When I met Marge, I mentioned that I was writing a book. She said, "I know the name of your book. It's *Wisdom . . . through the Ages* or something like that?" The name of my book was *Wisdomism,* and I was completely amazed. She said that she had developed psychic abilities. She hired me and I began working for her, bringing in some much-needed cash.

— Chapter Sixteen —

I met and moved in with a man on our first date. It was crazy. The relationship was crazy. For a short time, we were engaged to be married. The bad times outweighed the good times.

After a year of care-giving, Dolly was stricken with chest pains and had to be admitted to the hospital. Sensing that the end was near, she asked to be transferred to Los Angeles to be with her son and other daughter. I helped to make the arrangements. She was eventually placed in hospice, where she died peacefully.

I was able to take some time off work and finish *Wisdomism*, the book that I'd started writing while I was in Cincinnati with Cathy. A few publishers responded to a well-written query letter and requested my final manuscript. In the end, the query letter turned out to be better than the manuscript, and the book was never published. I still felt in my heart that I was meant to write a book containing spiritual wisdom. The time had not yet arrived. The relationship with the man came to an abrupt end. It was time to go back to work and find another place to live.

I placed an ad offering organizing services on a bulletin board. Donna, a psychiatrist who worked from her residence, hired me to organize her entire home. I began working for her right away.

I found a room for rent through the local newspaper. A single guy in his forties with a two-bedroom, two-bath unit on the second floor of an older apartment complex was my new roommate. I didn't want a roommate, but it was more affordable than other options. I had my own bedroom and bathroom for the first time in a while. Given the stress from the relationship I'd just ended, I'd been neglecting my healthy eating style and had regained some of the weight I'd lost. My clothes were tight, some too tight to wear. I was looking forward to starting my healthy lifestyle anew. Thanks to my new client, I was able to buy all the furnishings I needed to be comfortable in my new place. I longed for nothing more than peace and quiet.

Much to my chagrin—actually, I was totally pissed off—as soon as I moved in, my new roommate, Sal, told me that his teenage daughter would be visiting for three weeks. One of the reasons I had rented this room was because Sal worked five days a week, from eleven in the morning until seven at night. I figured his schedule would give me plenty of time to be by myself. It was too late for me to do anything now—I'd paid the rent and was all moved in. First the daughter arrived. Then a twenty-year-old stripper, a former roommate of Sal's, showed up and planted herself in his bed. She decided to become Sal's girlfriend. Sal bought her a new cell phone, let her use his car, and gave her money for food and whatever she needed. She cooked up a scheme where she would go to Las Vegas to dance and earn some big bucks. She ordered hundreds of dollars' worth of clothes from Victoria's Secret and charged it to Sal's credit card. She convinced Sal to pay for her breast augmentation operation too. I knew that she was insincere about being Sal's girlfriend, but he was caught—hook, line, and sinker.

By Christmastime I was living with a man, his teenage daughter, and a twenty-year-old stripper. They bought a Christmas tree, decorated it, and were having a good ole time. I turned my room into a little mini-apartment and kept to myself as much as possible. I was still hurting over the end of my recent engagement—a cherished dream that had slowly disintegrated. I felt alone and broken. But I knew that being with a partner for the wrong reasons was like constantly being slapped in the face with my own neuroses.

Stripper-girl refused to clean up after herself. She left dirty dishes in the sink and spilled food on the floor. I was the only one who seemed to be interested in taking out the stinking trash. She also brought with her two cats, whose litter box stunk up the whole apartment, and they were allowed to climb all over the counters with their little shit-digging paws. I love cats with all my heart, but not their hair and poop where I eat my food. Nor did I wish to take care of someone else's cat's litter box. After Stripper-girl's surgery she was up at all hours in pain, making noise and using my bathtub.

Not surprisingly, things went from bad to worse. She was not a week out of her breast surgery when she began secretly seeing another man. She phoned him while I was there and Sal was at work. She confronted me about putting the cats into the bedroom and shutting the door while she was out with her new boobs and new boyfriend. She became very angry and was nasty to both Sal and me. I decided that enough was enough and it was time to move out. I went to see Sal at work the next day and gave him a thirty-day notice. He said he didn't want me to leave but understood. Then he asked me what I thought about Stripper-girl—he had a bad feeling about her. I told him about the man.

That night when I came home, she was gone for good. He apparently told her to call the man she was seeing to come and pick her up. She tried to deny it. He said, "I can't believe you would do that to us." She said, "There was no us," and left. He was crushed. He threw the sexy clothes he'd bought her in the Dumpster and returned the ones she hadn't worn. But he couldn't get the breast implants back, or all the money he'd spent on her, though he believed that she'd repay him someday. From that moment on Sal spent all of his time shut up in his room watching television, leaving only to go to work. I pretty much did the same thing in my room, except I wasn't working. I could not find enough organizing work to pay the rent. Sal let me slide—I think because of all the turmoil with Stripper-girl.

A trial date was set for Cathy regarding her misuse of company funds; at the same time she was going through her third divorce. She was living with a new man at the time who was sticking by her. In the end, Cathy was sentenced to a term of one year. The court allowed her to begin her sentence the following October, after her youngest daughter graduated from college and the oldest one was married, so that she could attend the ceremonies. Our brother Michael, along with the rest of us, was quite upset that Cathy was going to prison. None of us could believe that it was actually happening. Cathy distanced herself from me. I tried to be a friend to her in a time of need, to no avail. We just drifted farther and farther apart. She eventually served almost ten months in a federal prison.

I was doing my best to move on. I felt inspired to write to *The Oprah Winfrey Show* about my idea to form a panel of spiritual teachers and create a unified network of resources for public use, for the purpose of healing through wisdom and truth. I wrote to Neale Donald Walsch and a few others with my idea, asking them if they'd be agreeable to participating in such a show. Mr. Walsch answered me personally and said that he'd be available. After several months and numerous letters and emails to Oprah with no response, I finally gave up. I had, however, started a dialogue with Mr. Walsch through email. He was forming a group at the time called Humanity's Team and planning a conference in Oregon. I wanted to attend but wasn't sure how I'd be able to afford to travel there.

Mr. Walsch had a poll on his website asking if his readers agreed or disagreed with the statement: "Organized religions are a major problem in the world today." Most people agreed with the statement; I was one of the few who did not. In one of my emails, I jokingly made the comment that he must have been testing to see who was awake out here, and that of course I did not see organized religion as a major part of the world's problems. Mr. Walsch emailed me back and told me that he was very serious about organized religion being a problem, and went on to list many of the reasons why.

I felt bad. I thought that maybe I had offended him. I emailed him back, explaining that it was through his teachings that I was able to see that our conflicts were not out there, but only existed within. I stated that organized religion was no more of a problem than government, pollution, healthcare, and education. I explained that all of these things were not the cause of our problems but rather the effect of them. The change would need to come from the level of cause, which is the mind. As he had so eloquently stated in his teachings, our only real problem is us imagining that we are separate from God and from each other. I explained that it was through his teachings that I'd been awakened to these truths.

I'd recommended his books countless times over the years. Many of his teachings have served me well over the years and contributed greatly to my continued spiritual awakening. I was grateful to him for having the courage to be a spark that became a fire that changed everything. Because of him, I was able to keep my spark alive long enough to get to a place where it would blaze into a fire that would change everything.

As time passed, my ideas for *The Oprah Winfrey Show* became a memory. I hadn't paid Sal rent for over three months and couldn't afford to leave. The bills from Stripper-girl started piling up, and Sal

needed the money. I went to an employment agency for domestic help and was hired by a wealthy South African family to keep house and cook for the elderly parents of the family. They lived in an exclusive, luxury high-rise apartment in La Jolla. In addition to a weekly salary, I was provided with my own one-bedroom fully furnished condominium. It was beautiful, with marble countertops, bath and kitchen; stone floors; high-end window coverings; and state-of-the-art appliances, including a washer and dryer. I had never lived in such opulence. They even installed a little desk, with file drawers built in, to a little room off of the kitchen, because they knew I was a writer. I was thrilled!

Before moving into the condo, I called Michael several times, leaving messages for him but never getting a call back. Cathy's oldest daughter was getting married in September, and I planned to buy an airline ticket for my brother. I wanted to confirm the dates and times with him. I waited impatiently to get phone service installed so that I could talk to Michael and make our plans to attend the wedding. Each day they promised it would happen. Each day I would get home and have no dial tone.

About a week after I moved into the condo, I was making my lunch in the kitchen of my employer's home. The woman was out at a doctor's appointment. The man was home, and when he came into the kitchen he was disturbed to see that I was making my lunch there, which I'd been doing every day since I'd started. Two days later, the parents and their son met with me in their living room. The son informed me that the father had decided he didn't want full-time help and that I was being relieved of my duties. They told me that I'd done an excellent job and would receive a high recommendation. They gave me a check for one thousand dollars and promised another similar check when I moved out of the condo. They would provide a mover to move me to my new place. I was crying. I couldn't help it. I couldn't believe it. I'd just

moved and unpacked all my things. They loaned me a cell phone so that I could start looking for another job and sent me home.

Despite this upheaval in my life, I was still very worried about my brother. The next morning, I called Mom. I told her that I'd been trying to call Michael for a couple of weeks, but he never answered his phone. She'd been trying to reach him too, to get his jacket size so she could buy him one for the wedding. I told her that if I were able to reach him I'd ask. I knew that Michael had moved into a little efficiency motel room and was making a decent wage working as a full-time maintenance man for a nightclub. He worked hard six days a week and spent most of his off-time relaxing in his little room. I'd sent him a picture of me at Moonlight Beach, and he'd told me that it sat on his dresser. I'd also sent him some pictures of us as kids.

Less than an hour after I hung up from Mom there was a knock at my door. The elderly man for whom I had been working was standing there. He told me to call Mom, that there had been a death in the family. When I called her back, she said that Michael was dead. A homicide detective from Dallas had called and told her. Michael's body had been found in his room; I wasn't told what he died of. I couldn't believe it—my brother was dead. He wouldn't be attending the wedding. He wouldn't see his son. He wouldn't see his granddaughter. I cried and cried.

I was just starting to figure out how to wake up each morning without thinking about killing myself. I was just learning to feel happy. When I caught myself falling to pieces, I stopped. I decided right then and there that I couldn't afford to fall apart. I'd spent too much of my life sad. I decided that I'd experience death differently this time. I immediately made arrangements to fly to Erie where he was to be buried.

I'd not been able to talk to him one last time, but almost immediately I began to hear Michael communicate with me in my inner mind's ear. He told me that he was alive, and not in a different location, only a different state of being. At first, I was not sure if the communication was real. Over time, I came to know and trust that it was indeed real. I learned to relinquish my attachment to experiencing him through my five senses in the physical world. I developed a different relationship with him that made it possible to stay connected in the nonphysical one.

I telephoned the hotel where Michael lived and spoke with the manager. He told me that apparently Michael had started hanging out with a woman who came to work at the club. People warned him to stay away from her because she was bad news. Michael had been found in his room, lying on the bathroom floor, with a needle in his arm. He said that Michael must not have been back using long because he had paid his rent on time every week. The police suspected that the dosage he injected through the needle might've been tainted and were investigating. *What difference does it make?* I thought. He was gone, and nothing was going to bring him back. I believed that he was so worn down and disillusioned by life that he just gave up. Shooting up was his way of escaping. Only this time, the lethal mixture made his escape permanent.

After I heard the news of Michael's death, none of my other problems, including my lost job and condo, seemed important. I walked around La Jolla, thinking that if I still drank, I sure would have needed a few right about then. But I didn't drink anymore. Even under these circumstances, I wasn't tempted. I smiled to myself, realizing how very much I had changed. Having a drink was only a passing thought, and nothing more.

I made my way to Erie. Mom was beside herself and numb with grief. We all were. We had known for a long time that this day would arrive, but still we were not prepared. No one ever is. It was unbelievable that we were going through this with another sibling. Michael dead at the age of fifty from a drug overdose. Both our brothers were gone, along with our father. All the males of our family were buried side by side. From her grief, the stress of her own troubled life, and continued alcohol abuse Cathy appeared to have aged ten years. I wanted to cry just looking at her.

I recalled how hard Beej had been on Michael and thought that he probably never really had a chance in this world. What would become of the rest of us? Only time would tell. John Lennon, "Imagine."

I returned to California and found a little efficiency apartment in Cardiff, a small community twenty minutes north of La Jolla and just south of Encinitas. As promised, my employers gave me another one thousand dollars and provided a mover. Fortunately, my former roommate had stored my furniture for me. It was perfect for my new place. I spread some of Michael's ashes at my favorite Moonlight Beach, near the place where I always meditated and visited with Jesus. I had kept my promise to Michael to bring him out to California, but not at all how I'd imagined. I began writing a book about life after death, as told by Michael.

I flew east for my oldest niece's wedding. She married the boyfriend she'd been dating since the ninth grade. It was a lovely ceremony. They were married late in the afternoon in a little church across the street from the beach. My niece was the most beautiful bride I'd ever seen, and the groom was very handsome in his tuxedo. They were clearly very much in love. Their fairy-tale wedding was followed by a huge sit-down dinner and reception. The next day Mom, Howard, and I met Cathy, her boyfriend, and my youngest niece for breakfast. I flew back to California filled with happy memories.

A few weeks later when I saw a picture of myself at the wedding, I decided to stop bleaching my hair. Suddenly, I thought the color looked hideous, so I let it grow out from that moment on. I'd been coloring my hair for so many years I didn't even know what its real color was! When the roots had grown out a few inches, my hairstylist asked if I'd like to add some color just while it was growing out. I said no thank you. For years and years, if the roots were showing even the littlest bit, I came unglued. Now I was just the opposite.

I couldn't find enough organizing work to support myself, so I soon secured a live-in caregiver position through the same agency that had placed me in La Jolla. My friend Ben, whom I knew from my first days in California, helped me move into my new home, a pleasant two-story townhouse. The son of an elderly woman named Kathleen hired me. I cleaned and reorganized the entire house before Kathleen came home from an extended stay at a nursing home. She was becoming increasingly frail and was beginning to suffer from a form of dementia. The dementia was not too bad yet, but it was escalating. I had my own bedroom and bath upstairs. Kathleen slept downstairs in the living room.

As soon as I was paid, I went to Cilantro Live! a raw food restaurant that I'd wanted to visit for several months. I drove about forty-five minutes south, past downtown San Diego. The moment I read the menu and ordered an entrée, I was hooked. I introduced myself to Cristina Guzman, the owner, and started going there every Saturday and Sunday. That was my treat to myself; Cilantro Live! was the only restaurant I went to. I had simply lost my appetite for many of the foods I used to eat. I'd gone back and forth from eating vegetarian and vegan style over the past few years. Now I was drawn to the all organic, raw, and vegan foods.

Cilantro Live! had the most delicious food I'd ever tasted. I began to buy and read books on raw food preparation. Now that I could afford it, I began buying the necessary equipment. I always loved being in the kitchen, and I learned a whole new way to prepare food. The weight I'd regained caused by stress and not eating healthily started to come off again. Kathleen watched as I prepared many new and delicious foods. She didn't eat raw food, but she enjoyed watching me work with it. I taught her how to prepare it and told her the information was for use in her next life, and she laughed. I cooked all of her favorite foods—mashed potatoes, meatloaf, chicken, and spaghetti with meatballs—but I only ate the raw foods I prepared. I never felt deprived with my new style of eating. As I was naturally drawn to it, at the same time my long-time food addictions and cravings started to disappear. I craved succulent tomatoes, crispy cucumber, crunchy onions, juicy peaches, plums, pears, exotic papayas and mangos. Sunshine, life-force-infused food!

As I continued to practice daily meditation and continually worked on healing my inner self, I adapted new healthful appetites and behaviors, which were symbolic of and in sync with the new healthful thoughts of my mind. I observed that it was through my spiritual awakening that my old destructive behaviors and appetites fell away from me, and in their stead appeared new, life-promoting behaviors and appetites, making them my freedoms rather than my disciplines. There was no magic formula; as I focused on my inner work and spiritual awakening my outer world changed in significant and positive ways, including my thoughts, words, and deeds. I made the inner changes and observed the outer changes occur easily, effortlessly, and automatically. As much as I'd wanted and craved candy bars and cheese puffs, I now wanted a beautiful Heirloom tomato. Miraculous freedom!

Our most health-giving foods are rich in nutrients and life-force energy, which are supplied by the elements of our planet: earth, air, water, and sun. Was it so far out of the realm of possibility to consider that our physical bodies could advance enough that we'd be able to take in these elements some way other than through "food," as we know it? Was it possible that we could fuel our bodies by somehow naturally absorbing the elements, thereby cutting out the middleman (food)?

I transitioned to a totally raw diet over a two-month period. I felt and looked the best I ever had; even so, after one year my job was taking a toll on me. Kathleen's needs were ever-increasing. Her dementia worsened to the point that I told the family I needed to move out. I was willing to care for her on weekdays, but I had to live somewhere else. She needed twenty-four-hour care and her family could not afford it, so they moved her into a nursing home.

I moved to an apartment in Encinitas, within walking distance of Moonlight Beach. I wanted very badly to finish my book about my communications with Michael after his death. I was torn between writing and earning rent money. I tried to find organizing jobs, but it seemed like there was no work like that around. So I kept writing. I figured that I might as well write rather than sit around.

By this time I was growing my own wheat grass and making all my own food, except for my outings to Cilantro Live! When Cristina discovered I was out of work, she refused to let me pay for my meals. Cristina, along with her husband and daughter, continually asked about my book and encouraged me to keep writing. Cristina told me to get cards made and to start teaching raw-food preparation; so I did. I certainly never set out to have a career as a raw-food chef, it just happened. Soon I was teaching classes in my kitchen.

Still, I was struggling financially. It was a very difficult time for me. I felt torn, one side wanting to write, and the other side afraid of not being able to survive. I continued to see the flashes of iridescent indigo light from time to time. I had a vision of my fully-grown adult self traveling through this huge birth canal and simultaneously giving birth myself. It was an extraordinary vision and feeling. Somehow I managed to have enough to eat, even though eviction proceedings had started. There was a whole process of papers being served and a court date being set. If I could come up with the money at almost any point, I would be able to stop the eviction. I was desperately trying to make that happen.

I continued to walk on the beach nearly every day and view as many sunsets as possible that summer. I meditated each morning and night. One particular day, I went to Cilantro Live! to eat earlier in the day. As evening turned to night, I watched a movie on television. Then I meditated on my couch before going to bed. It was a Saturday night about eleven or twelve. I was sitting on my couch and I must have dozed off, because I suddenly woke up to someone standing right in front of me in my living room. There was a large ottoman between me and the person in front of me. I wasn't scared, but I was startled because I lived alone and I hadn't let anyone in the apartment. As I tried to focus on the face, it faded from view.

This all happened in less than a split second, yet I will never forget that face. I have often easily visualized many things throughout all of my life. I've had many vivid dreams; some of them coming true, and some of them quite real. I'd already had my share of unusual occurrences. But never anything like this. This was here in this tangible real world, not in my mind. I saw this being as clearly as I could see my hand in front of my face.

The being looked like a person, though semitransparent. There was a body and a head. I could see the head and face most clearly. I really don't recall what the "body" looked like or what clothes, if any, were worn. The face was that of a very ordinary, plain man. He had brown-black hair and a beard. Both were meticulously well-trimmed and groomed. The beard was very close to his face. His eyes were green, or possibly brown. He had a light-colored complexion. He was there and gone before I knew what had really happened. After the vision faded from view I asked the empty space, "Who are you?" I heard in my mind's ear, "I am Jesus. I am real and you are not alone."

I went to bed and fell into a deep sleep. The next morning when I woke up it wasn't until I meditated that I recalled seeing Jesus. I thought that if Jesus had been in my living room, then anything was possible and life would work out somehow. I had not ever had a vision like that before. Jesus' words touched me deeply and profoundly. For most of my life I had felt utterly alone; his assurance had tremendous significance to me at that moment, just as I am sure Jesus knew it would. From that moment on I knew that I was never alone. Someday, maybe, I'd try to paint a picture of that face.

Shortly after this extraordinary vision, I began the practice of sun-gazing, which was taught to me by a man from India named Hira Ratan Manek. I was told that sun-gazing would further purify and heal my body while assisting me in my spiritual awakening. It became a form of meditation for me, and I continued the practice steadily for fifteen months, working my way up from ten seconds, then adding ten more seconds each day until reaching a full forty-four minutes. Sun-gazing was only done during the first or last hour of sunlight of the day, when there were zero UV rays.

The total experience of sun-gazing changed me in some indefinable way. The practice seemed to improve me, mentally, physically, and spiritually. Sun-gazing, for me, was symbolic of a decision to heal, which I made at the level of cause, the mind. What appear to be healthy habits and healthy bodies are symbols of a healthy mind. As I cleansed and healed physically and mentally, my body required less and less energy or fuel. I became naturally drawn to higher-quality whole foods, which provided my body with excellent nutrition and fuel. I remembered quite well when I couldn't imagine how I'd live without alcohol, cigarettes, and cheese puff dinners. Now I couldn't imagine how my body actually survived all of that self-destruction.

It was truly amazing that my appetites and behaviors changed as they did. As I awakened and returned to what I truly am, I needed less and less of everything. As long as I was here, I would still have work to do, but I noticed that I was progressing and my outer life appeared to mirror that progress. I did not forcibly or consciously change my behaviors and appetites in order to awaken. As I awakened, I observed and experienced miraculous and amazing behavior and appetite changes, which occurred unconsciously, easily, and effortlessly.

As I awakened, I also became more and more drawn to nature. Perhaps nature is simply symbolic of our closeness to God. Certainly we've all heard this expressed, or have expressed and felt it for ourselves. I didn't spend more and more of my time close to nature in order to feel good and be close to God. As I awakened, I became closer to God and was therefore naturally drawn to spend more and more time close to nature. I also felt more at peace from within, and closer and more connected to all others.

Perhaps our beautiful sun and L. Frank Baum's brilliant yellow brick road in the classic childhood story, *The Wonderful Wizard of Oz*, are merely symbols guiding us back to the awareness of our own beautiful and brilliant inner light. I can still hear and feel the longing and rich deepness of Dorothy's words, "There's no place like Home, there's no place like Home," which she repeated while clicking the heels of her ruby slippers and awakening from the dream of Oz. Will we awaken one day and find that we already are that which we've all along been seeking?

⁓

The time had come to send query letters to various publishers about the new book I'd written about my brother's life after death. This time I wrote only to publishers that had done books by or about the spiritual teachers I admired. Bob Friedman of Hampton Roads Publishing Company, who'd published Neale Donald Walsch's first books, was at the top of my list. I emailed my query letter to him as well as fifteen or twenty other publishers. Mr. Friedman responded the next morning, inviting me to send a copy of my manuscript to him for review. I was elated and sent him a copy immediately.

While I was waiting to hear back from them, Cathy finished serving her time and was released from prison. Starting over, she was optimistic and hopeful. I was so relieved that she was safe. Not a day went by that I wasn't worried about her while she was in prison. We'd written every week and had begun to rebuild our relationship, little by little.

One bright sunny morning after taking my daily beach walk, I went to the grocery store to buy a few items. The young woman who always posted my organizing service advertisements on the bulletin board told me that she was out of them. I thanked her and told her I'd bring some more in. After my beach walk the next day, I brought the advertisements to the grocery store. My helper said, "Oh I was mistaken, I still have plenty of your ads." I thanked her, but as I returned to my car, I remembered that I needed to check on something in the store.

As I walked back toward the store, a very tall, well-built, handsome mailman crossed my path and said hello to me. I instantly felt a very strong and noticeable attraction to him—a very rare thing for me to experience. I returned his greeting. He continued on his way and I did too. Then, suddenly, I turned around, and at the same instant he did too. By that time we were pretty far apart. I stopped walking and he turned and walked toward me; and we met on the sidewalk in front of the store.

We introduced ourselves and began talking. I had no makeup on, my hair was pulled back, and I smelled of dried-up sweat and the beach. He didn't seem to notice. I told him that I went to Moonlight Beach regularly to walk and was there most evenings to watch the sunset. He asked if he could meet me there sometime. I gave him one of my flyers and he called me a day or two later. His name was Rod.

While watching the sunset together, he told me that he was a recovering alcoholic and was divorced with two children. One was grown and the other nearly grown. He attended AA meetings on a regular basis. It had been a year since he had stopped drinking and a couple of years since his divorce. After the sunset, I invited him to see where I lived and offer him a snack. I showed him my "raw kitchen." He commented that he thought that was a very healthy way to eat and, although he did not eat that way, it was the way to go. After a snack and some more conversation, we said goodnight. Rod called me a few times but never asked me out on a date. He just came over after his AA meetings. I thought that maybe he couldn't afford to take me out, so I invited him over for dinner.

I told him a story about how twenty years earlier a woman told my fortune. She was known to be pretty accurate and said, among other things, that my soul mate was Ra, the Egyptian God of the Sun. His full name was Rana-dodd. She explained that my soul mate in this life wouldn't have the same exact name, but a similar-sounding name. Rod's full name was eerily close to Rana-dodd.

After dinner, Rod wanted to make out and I wanted to talk. He wasn't interested in talking. I put on some music, Brian Kennedy's "Crazy Love," and pulled him off the couch to dance. He kept trying to make out with me. When I finally put an end to it, he said goodnight and went home. I didn't hear from him again. I meditated about Rod. I was told that Rod would have a major spiritual awakening later. I knew that, at least for now, he and I were not meant to be. There was no doubt about it—I was definitely changing.

After six months in my apartment, the eviction was finally going to happen. I was unable to pay my rent. The date of my required vacancy had been set. I met a woman about my age named Sarah through an advertisement I placed about raw-food preparation classes. We'd been hanging out together while I was being evicted from my apartment, and she told me about a place where I might live. I couldn't figure out what to do.

A couple of days before I had to be out of the apartment, I called Mike, a friend who owned a truck. Mike had come into my life one day when I had a flat tire on my bike and he fixed it for me at a local gas station. Another time, when I had no food, he brought me a big bucket of tangerines from his brother's ranch and gave me some money for gas and food. He always seemed to be there just when I needed help. He reminded me of my brother Michael, and I believed that Michael had sent him to help me.

I had to move out on a Sunday. Mike and I had a storage unit lined up, and he was scheduled to bring his truck over at noon on Sunday. I began packing. Sarah came over early Sunday morning to take me to see a little cottage in Carlsbad, about fifteen minutes north. We went over, and after peeking in windows and making a nuisance of ourselves, we met with the woman who owned the cottage. It was in the middle of her forested, fairy-like backyard. It wasn't very big, the size of an efficiency apartment. It was vacant, quiet, and clean. My furniture would fit perfectly.

She wanted five hundred dollars per month, which was cheap. I was broke, but a big client, Donna, had called me the night before and hired me for a couple of weeks. I explained my situation to the landlady, who said no problem. I didn't have to give her a deposit, and I could wait until December to start paying the rent. She said I could move in that day. We met Mike back at my apartment, and instead of moving my things into storage and me living in my car again, he moved me into the little cottage. It was a Thanksgiving miracle I could hardly believe.

After settling in, I called Rod one day, to check to see if he had done any awakening. He wanted to come over and have sex with me. I told him that was not going to happen. After his call, I started thinking about his request. I became angry. I called him back and was connected to his voice mail. I asked him if he really thought that he was just going to come over and have sex with me. I told him that I thought that sex was his new alcohol. He'd shown no respect or honor for either of us. Later, when I returned, there was an angry voice mail back from him. In his message he said something along the lines of how dare I say that to him? I didn't know him or anything about his life, and I had no right to judge him. Maybe I should stop sun-gazing and get a job so I could pay the rent.

I know he didn't mean it to be funny, but I couldn't help laughing. I called him back and was able to speak to him personally. He started in with, "How dare you, how dare you," in his thick Boston accent. I told him he was right, I had no right to judge him. I told him that I really wanted someone with whom to share my life. I just wanted to get to know him before anything physical happened, to see what if anything would naturally develop. I told Rod that I was a work in progress and still did not have all the answers, and I apologized. He calmed down and told me that we were all trying to find answers. He said that I'd talked suggestively to him and egged him on. I told him that I was just trying to make light of his attempts to get me to have sex with him. I told him that he was a very attractive, well-built man, and that I was tempted, but in the end that a meaningless sexual relationship was not what I wanted. I apologized again if I'd led him on. I told him I liked going to a little coffee shop in Encinitas and, if he ever wanted to meet for coffee or tea and maybe start a friendship, to give me a call.

It felt good to not do or be what someone else wanted me to do or be. I had turned a corner and made a major shift in my life. No longer would I settle by putting a man's sexual needs ahead of my own well-being. Marvin Gaye, "Sexual Healing." That was an even more significant moment than I realized at the time. I never saw or heard from Rod again. Some God of Sun he turned out to be—more like a pagan dog!

One morning, just as I was waking up, I saw and heard two beings in my mind. They looked like ET beings. They told me that one of them was me, from the future, and they were there to help guide me through to a different outcome in this lifetime. They didn't say who the second being was or is. They asked me if I wanted help getting my book published, and I answered eagerly, "Yes!" They suggested that I call Bob Friedman at Hampton Roads Publishing and ask whether he'd ever heard of sun-gazing. So I called Bob and asked him that very question. He said, "Yes, I have a friend who practices it." I was taken aback. I was not expecting that he'd say yes; I was just following the ETs' advice.

Bob and I talked a bit about my manuscript, which he'd had for a few months and hadn't yet read. Lisette, who also worked at Hampton Roads, called me later that same day. She said that she was the friend of Bob Friedman's who practiced sun-gazing, which is what she'd called to discuss. She asked about my manuscript, located it and read it, then passed it on to Bob. She told me that Bob would get back to me when he was done reading it.

I meditated and thanked God in advance for sending me a way to work consistently and in a way that would be enjoyable to me. I thanked God as if I already had this and placed myself in a state of gratitude. Then two calls came in rapid succession. First, my former clients from North Carolina contacted me and asked me to come out to do some organizing for them. Second, I was contacted by a hospital in Mexico for a job I'd interviewed for several months before. Several months prior, Cristina told me about a regular customer, Abby, who worked as a colonic therapist and instructor at a state-of-the-art hospital in Mexico. She'd asked Cristina if she knew anyone who was a raw-food chef whom she could recommend for a job opening at the hospital. Cristina thought of me immediately and told the woman that she would ask me if I was interested. I told Cristina, "Yes!" I contacted Abby, who after talking with me arranged an interview with the hospital.

Abby championed me from the start. I loved her right away. She only wanted to do good things in this world, and she believed in me enough to help me. When I arrived at the hospital on the morning of the interview, she showed me around. This hospital was unique. It was located on a cliff overlooking the ocean. Every single room faced the ocean and had a beautiful view. The teaching kitchen was fabulous, with a huge island in the middle and several stations for hands-on teaching. Every single guest room had marble bathrooms, the most comfortable beds ever, and huge floor-to-ceiling sliding glass doors. The entire building was beautifully decorated with fine art and beautiful fabrics.

I was to interview that afternoon and then spend the night as their guest. They were looking for someone to fill the position of nutritionist, raw-food chef, and instructor. I went through the interview and shared my meals in the guest dining room with Abby. She said that my interview was progressing well, but that they were concerned that I didn't have a college degree in nutrition. The person hired would be working closely with the doctors who'd make their recommendations. Plus there were certain menus designed to meet the dietary needs of the various ailments that needed to be followed. It was something that anyone with any brains could handle.

Abby commented that Jesus didn't have a degree, so why were degrees so important? With my raw-food preparation and knowledge, I had valuable and much-needed hands-on experience that they didn't even teach in a college. I slept comfortably and drove back to Carlsbad the next day. Later, I emailed them and thanked them for the interview for that position, which I considered the opportunity of a lifetime. They never responded. A week went by. I sent another email. Nothing. Then I called. Finally, the head of human resources spoke to me and asked what my salary requirements were and said they would be in touch.

I started receiving colonics from a therapist in Abby's clinic in San Diego. I brought my therapist some of the raw food that I'd made. She loved it. Abby saw what I'd brought and took some of it down to the hospital to show the doctors. I hadn't heard anything further when Abby called me and spoke to me about how I needed to really go after this job if it was what I really wanted. When she said that, something in me snapped. I told Abby that I'd chased after many things in my life and it had gotten me exactly nowhere. I told her that what I wanted more than a particular sum of money was for them to want me as much as I wanted them. I told her firmly that I no longer wished to pursue the position.

Several months later, when the degreed nutritionist they'd hired hastily departed, the hospital contacted me asking if I was still interested in the position. When I responded that I was, the head of human resources asked how much money I wanted. By the next day I was told that I'd be hired *and* at the amount I'd requested. I would begin a whole new career upon returning from my organizing job in North Carolina, plus I had a publisher reading my manuscript. Things were looking much brighter.

I flew to North Carolina and was paid well for my services. After I'd been there a couple of days, I received a message from Bob Friedman at Hampton Roads. Their reputation as a publisher was excellent, and they'd published many fine books on spirituality; I knew it would be an honor to be one of their authors. When I returned his call, he said, "Your book needs a lot of work before it is publishable, in my opinion." Well, that was better news than being flat-out rejected, as I had been by a number of publishers, most of whom hadn't even read my manuscript. At least there was some hope. Was he saying my book "*could* be publishable"?

I asked Mr. Friedman if he'd be willing to help me and give me some guidance. He said, "I might, but that could be done through email." I thanked Mr. Friedman for taking the time to read my manuscript. Lisette spoke with me again briefly and told me not to be concerned if they rejected my book. She told me that about seventy publishers had rejected Dr. Seuss before he was finally published. She was so kind and encouraging. Because of her, I'd connected with Mr. Friedman and a relationship was initiated. Those ET beings knew what they were doing!

A night or two before I was scheduled to fly back to California, the women I'd worked for over the past week took me out to dinner. They were all drinking and offered me a taste, but I only felt like drinking water. I'd truly lost my desire for alcohol and all mind-altering substances. It was a little strange for them—the last time they'd seen me I was sipping on chocolate martinis, margaritas, and champagne. It was good to see them all. We laughed and talked the night away.

Once I returned home to California, I started looking for a place to live. I decided to return to the small beach community where I'd lived with my ex fiancé, which was forty minutes closer to Mexico. There were too many apartments from which to choose.

I meditated on it that night, and the next morning I thanked God in advance for providing me with the perfect place to live. I went back to my cottage and started answering advertisements from the classifieds. By the second to last phone call I made, I knew I was talking to the woman who would be my new landlady.

The apartment was three blocks from the beach. It was a nice-sized studio in an older complex. I told Carol, the manager, that my credit was so bad that the last time they ran a credit check the eastern part of the United States had blacked out for several days. She told me to come over anyway and take a look at the apartment. Her husband, Mel, showed me the unit. I liked it right away. They told me that as long as I could pay the rent, the apartment was mine. I put down a deposit and went home to get packed. I loved my new apartment. It had everything I needed. Carol and Mel were the best landlords I ever had. They immediately made me feel right at home and did everything they could to make me comfortable. A warm friendship started to develop.

I still had my 1995 Cougar, but I used my bike as much as possible. There was a grocery store within biking distance and a farmers' market every week just two blocks from where I lived. The town, a small, close-knit friendly community, was right on the beach with only one major road leading into the area, so traffic was mostly local and fairly light. I rode my bike every day when I wasn't working in Mexico. Hampton Roads sent me an official rejection letter, and so did several other publishers. I wasn't too discouraged. No one was offering to publish my book, so I self-published it.

My teaching job at the hospital in Mexico was going well. I received many positive comments on my classes. The food classes, complete with samples, were an automatic hit. In the sprouting class I told the story about how unhealthy my habits used to be, and how I knew that many of these students were facing serious health challenges. I told them that I knew very well that this new way of food preparation could be overwhelming. I told them that they would learn and be provided with the knowledge and tools they'd need in order to return home and continue with their new and healthy eating program.

I developed a packet I called the Kitchen Corner, which was based upon the needs of most guests. It provided resources and nutritional information as well as recipes. I consulted with guests between classes and often shared meals with them in the guest dining room. A few times, I received applause at the end of my classes. It was the most fun, fulfilling, and rewarding job of my life. Every Sunday around noon after my second class, I headed back home. I worked two-and-a-half days each week and earned enough income to comfortably support myself. Life was better than I'd ever imagined it could be.

— CHAPTER SEVENTEEN —

One month shy of my forty-eighth birthday I was fit, healthy, and a slender one-hundred-twenty-five pounds. I'd never looked or felt better in my life. My nephew Mike was getting married in July, one weekend before my thirtieth high school reunion. I took enough time off work to attend both.

I attended the first night of the reunion's festivities with my former sweetheart and classmate, Chris, with whom I'd stayed in touch over the years. He had recently married and was doing very well. Another classmate, Cal, met us at Chris's nearby house, and the three of us walked to the party together.

I talked and reconnected with more people than I ever had before, probably because I had created a life I was loving and enjoying. I told some of my classmates about my book, and the word quickly spread. Many asked if I had any books with me, which I did, and a book signing was hastily arranged for the picnic the next day. It was a very good night. I'd come a long way from the girl who smoked dope behind a locker. I suppose we all had, some farther than others.

Kevin showed up toward the end of the night. We talked and cleared the air from our last uncomfortable meeting and phone conversation. A group of us headed to the same bar we'd gone to at the last reunion five years earlier. Kevin gave me a ride there, but I didn't stay long. He asked if we could go somewhere to talk the next day, and I agreed. The next morning we drove out to a beach he'd visited often as a kid. From what he said, he'd had a very happy childhood. We took a long walk on the beach and talked about our lives as children, then about what had happened since we last met.

Eventually, Kevin asked me if I was okay. I told him that finally I was and that I was creating a life that I loved. I told him, and meant it, that I was at peace with myself and the world. He looked at me and said, "I have never seen anything like this before, but there is a huge bright light all around you." I couldn't see it, but it sounded pretty cool. He said that he could tell that I was at peace, and I could tell that he was not. I suggested that he forgive himself. I told him that he didn't have to continue to feel bad over what had happened anymore. Then we left; he had to be somewhere with his family.

Chris and his new family accompanied me to the picnic. When I arrived I saw Kevin, and he and his wife introduced me to their children. I brought some books with me and in between visiting with classmates I ended up signing and selling over thirty books. Kevin bought one of my books from me, which I signed. One classmate pulled me aside and spoke with grave concern about her daughter who'd been fighting a drug addiction. Because Michael had died from a drug overdose she was very interested to learn as much as she could, which naturally led to a long discussion about drug abuse within the family.

Toward the day's end I, along with several other women, climbed atop of one of the picnic tables and danced to The Commodores's "Brick House," one of my all-time favorite table-dancing songs. Our thirty-year reunion officially came to an end. I decided that I liked the reunions several thousand times better than I had ever liked high school.

I wanted to spend some time with Mom before Mike's wedding the following weekend. Mom picked me up at my friend Diane's house, where I was staying, and we went to the mall to buy something for Mike's daughter and my grandniece. We found two beautiful dresses that she instantly loved. Afterward, we went back to Mom's house, where she began pointing out all the mistakes I'd made in my life, as moms sometimes do. I sighed and told her that I was doing the best I could.

Suddenly, the floodgates opened and I spilled my guts to her. As I sat across the table from my mother, I told her all of the traumatic things that had ever happened to me. It had never once crossed my mind to confide in her, but I couldn't stop talking. I had no idea why I was telling her everything, but it was a huge release. I told her how horrible it had been to be molested by my uncle when I was a child. I told her that it was equally horrible to be fondled later by the hospital orderly. I told her that I'd started drinking and doing drugs when I was twelve years old. I told her that I'd felt depressed since I was a girl and had wanted to kill myself many, many times. I told her that at age thirteen I'd been gang-raped at a church dance by a group of boys. Mom asked me why I hadn't told her before. I told her because I'd thought I deserved it; I thought it was my fault. She couldn't understand why I hadn't trusted her.

I started to cry. I thought I'd cried my last tears over that night long ago, but there I was crying, not because of the rape, but because no one had protected me. I cried because I had always felt so alone in the world. I told her about the older married policeman and the abortion. I told her that I prostituted myself in my twenties to pay the rent. By this point she was crying too. I asked her if anything similar had ever happened to her; she said no. Then she hugged me, and we didn't speak any further. For a fleeting moment, I hoped that maybe now we'd have a chance to have a closer relationship. All those secrets had been a wall between us, and now the wall was gone.

I felt better, like a tremendous weight had been lifted from my shoulders. I felt awakened to something powerful within me. This moment was indeed one of the highest and clearest of my life. There was a huge shift inside me. I saw the world differently, for the first time. It felt good to not hide and to not have secrets.

Even if I'd told her about the rape when it happened, she and a thousand like her could not have reached me. This was the script of my life, my destiny, and for reasons to be discovered through healing, those experiences were mine to live.

The next day my sister Cathy arrived. The formal outdoor wedding took place in the evening outside a charming chapel. I wore a full-length, black, close-fitting dress with spaghetti straps; I was told many times I looked stunning. I *felt* stunning. My grand-niece looked like a little princess in her own small full-length white dress, with her hair in an updo. My nephew was very handsome and his bride quite beautiful. We moved inside for the reception where a DJ was getting set up. There was an open bar and a sit-down dinner. Later, at the reception, the DJ played Sister Sledge's "We Are Family" at my request. Cathy and I hit the dance floor.

Cathy didn't drink at the reception and looked like her younger self again. She'd been out of prison for a year and was putting her life back together. When Cathy and I were alone, I shared with her all the things I'd finally revealed to Mom about my past. Cathy knew about the rape, but we'd never discussed it. She'd known about the married policeman too. We were lying side by side on the guest-room bed when I told her that I had prostituted myself in my twenties. Her eyebrows shot up in surprise.

My sister told me that she also had been raped as a teenager. She was fourteen at the time and, like me, a virgin. The man who raped her was in his twenties, someone she had met at her high school. He was not a student, but he was young enough to pass as one and had blended in with the student body. That is how he was able to meet Cathy and ask her for a date. She snuck out and went on a date with him behind our parents' backs because of his age, knowing our parents wouldn't permit it. I remembered the guy, and when it happened, because she'd lied about baby-sitting. When she came home, our parents were waiting for her because they'd found out that she had not been baby-sitting.

The man and his friend had picked her up and driven her to a schoolyard. He took her for a walk to a secluded spot, pushed her down onto concrete, raped her, and drove her home. When she walked in the front door, our parents yelled at her for lying and immediately sent her to her room, grounding her. She had just suffered the most devastating trauma of her life and was so paralyzed by fear, shame, and guilt that she couldn't speak of it. Just like me.

She didn't tell anyone what had happened that night, though I'd felt for a long time that Cathy had been hiding something. When I asked her what was wrong, she said, "Nothing." For years it was always the same answer. When she was married to her first husband, she used to sit silently for hours with a blank look on her face, a million miles away. We had a term for this blank look—"the eyes that cannot see." I often felt like I was alone when she was in the same room with me. Sometimes she couldn't engage in a meaningful conversation with anyone.

Many years later, after she'd suffered silently for countless years, she finally told Mom. Cathy said Mom cried and hugged her. Over the years, Cathy and I had had our ups and downs; through it all, we'd always stuck by each other—no matter what. I thought of the time when I'd finished a manuscript and couldn't afford the postage to send it to a handful of selected publishers. Without my asking, Cathy had given me the money, at a time when she barely had enough herself. Maybe now we'd begin to get an inkling of who the other truly was. Maybe, just maybe.

After Cathy had shared her story with me, I realized how our common experience of rape had separated us from each other all these years. When she told me about her rape, I felt that she was finally letting her wall down. It helped me to understand her and myself, on a higher level. I understood why she seemed so far away all those years. When we are violated, it shatters us. Unless people have been through it, they can't understand what we are going through. They can't understand why we can't just snap out of it. They are perplexed and frustrated that we are injured and broken. They sometimes become angry with us for being unable to lead a healthy, balanced life. And we blame ourselves. We are convinced that it was our fault. We think that there is something wrong with us and that we are damaged beyond repair. We are filled with fear and are choked silent by it. The oppressive weight of deep guilt follows us wherever we go. We feel like we will never be safe or secure ever again. We feel worthless, like a piece of garbage that has been set out on the curb for disposal. We work frantically and desperately to hide by abusing drugs, eating too much, spending money we don't have, and/or stealing what does not belong to us. We'll try anything and everything to fill the gaping hole left by the trauma, often to the neglect of all else that is important, including our children and ourselves. We must seek and find that one perfect relationship that will validate and justify our existence. We allow others to violate and abuse us in our most intimate relationships. We do things we really don't want to do. No matter how hard and long we cry out to others to fill our needs, they cannot fix us. This causes us to react with anger toward the world and ourselves. Sometimes, we allow our children to be abused. We cannot protect and help them because we cannot help ourselves. We remain mute.

The very thing that had separated us had become a healing catalyst, bringing us together again and on a higher level, bringing us closer to God and our Oneness. I was once shattered and now I was becoming "One Again."

Mike and his new bride went off on their honeymoon, and Cathy and I returned to our respective homes. Mom prepared to return to Oregon. Our lives would never be the same. The healing had begun. We'd have our day in the sun. The Five Stairsteps, "Ooh Child."

— CHAPTER EIGHTEEN —

I had always believed that someday I would go to Hawaii. I loved my job at the hospital in Mexico, teaching and connecting with the people, but the commute had gotten old. Had the job been in San Diego, it would have been fantastic. Even given the punishing drive, it was a great job. Why did I feel compelled to leave? My car was paid off. I was current on all my other bills too, and was finally getting a little ahead. Why couldn't I be a normal person, happy staying in one place for a while? Whatever it was that had always pulled at me was stronger than ever before. In the past, I had blindly moved to run away from myself, but the move to California, and the move I was now contemplating to Hawaii, were moves toward myself. The decision to move came from my inner guidance. I yearned to be free. Material things were less and less important to me.

I decided to trust that my future would take care of itself. I decided to go ahead and move to Hawaii to write my next book— after that I'd see what came next. I had a vision of myself in a red Santa Claus bikini with a Santa hat, walking on the beach on Christmas day. Hawaii was where I wanted to be, to have the first Christmas in a long time where I could feel happy with my life. My mental state continued to improve. My periods of depression decreased in severity and duration. I gave away most of my possessions, selling only the big things. Every day I felt a stronger and stronger need to just let go. Every morning I went through my things to decide what else I could let go, because I needed less and less.

I worked out my two-week notice at the hospital and hugged everyone good-bye. I was sorry to leave; it was the closest I'd come to a job where I was afforded the space to simply be me. Just before I left for Hawaii, I contacted Bob Friedman of Hampton Roads Publishing by email. I told him that I'd made some revisions to my manuscript, that it wasn't perfect but I had self-published it anyway, and offered him a copy. I told him I was moving to Hawaii to write my next book. He promptly emailed back and requested a copy of my book. He asked how long I'd be in Hawaii, and how the sales of my book were going. I replied that I'd sold a few hundred copies and had no idea how long I'd be in Hawaii. I dropped a book in the mail to him just before I left.

I had reduced my worldly belongings to six suitcases. It was still WAAAAY too much, but it would take a few months of dragging all of it around with me to realize that. It was so obviously symbolic of all the emotional and mental baggage I had yet to forgive and release. How could I miss this sign?!

On the day of my departure to Kauai, my landlady Carol offered to transport me and my excessive baggage to the airport. She was like a mom to me in many ways, and I appreciated how she and her husband had watched over me in San Diego. She'd been the first person to buy a copy of my book, and she had loved it. I left my car with a man who said he'd sell it for me and mail me the money. I said my farewells to all my California friends and set off on a new adventure. There I was in the air, flying to the most remote place in the world, a tiny speck of an island in the South Pacific. I didn't even tell my family; I just took off. It was November 29, 2005.

A friend of mine named Steve, whom I knew from California, had moved to Hawaii, also known as the Big Island, a few months earlier. He told me that Kauai was his favorite place and mentioned a hostel there. I emailed my travel plans to him but got no response. As I was shuttled from the airport into the town of Kapaa, I was mesmerized by the landscape of my newfound tropical paradise. Miguel, the hostel manager, welcomed me to the island of Kauai and showed me to my dorm room. At twenty dollars per night, it was an affordable way to stay on the island on a budget.

The hostel was right across the street from the beach, an easy walk after breakfast. It was a new experience to look out over the ocean and watch the sunrise. The next day I was sitting at a covered picnic table and there was Steve. He did a double take before he realized it was me. He'd arrived from the Big Island the day before just a few hours before me. He was staying in the co-ed dorm and I was in the women's. He hadn't received my email telling him the date of my arrival because he hadn't checked his email in months. Steve offered to show me around in his rental car since he knew the island. We drove to its west side where he showed me the Waimea Canyon, which I nicknamed the baby grand canyon. There were many beautiful sites that he showed me, and it was easy to see why it was called paradise. One of the sites offered views of two magnificent waterfalls.

I decided that it would be fun to live without a car. I had always wanted to be free of the responsibility and stress of owning an automobile. Everyone hitchhiked all over the island, and it was a very acceptable practice. So one day I awkwardly stuck my thumb out. I was quickly picked up and delivered to my destination. After that I had no qualms about hitchhiking anywhere and everywhere. The bus service was not the best, and it was too infrequent.

Back on the mainland my car sold, and I used the money to buy a bike as a Christmas present to myself. I rode my new bike, walked, or hitchhiked, and didn't miss having a car at all. I felt good that I was responsible for one less car on the island. I was doing so much walking that I decided to go to a nearby Birkenstock store to buy some healthy footwear. I became fast friends with the manager, Sue. She sold me four pair of therapeutic sandals for better support for my feet, legs, and back. I joked I'd traded my car in for a bike and a pair of Birkenstocks. I rode my bike to the beach every day to walk and sunbathe.

One day I saw a woman named Melanie working at Papayas, the local health food store, and the next day she showed up in the bunk across from me. We hit it off right away; she'd just moved from Northern California. We listened to music together and talked. One day at the beach I met Chris, a man from San Francisco who was living in a tent while writing a book. I told him I was a writer and was in Hawaii to write a book too. Another new friendship began.

One afternoon I saw a notice for a dishwasher job at the local Mexican restaurant posted on the hostel bulletin board, and I immediately applied. Shelia, the owner—a big, tough, lumbering, cigarette-smoking woman—doubted that I'd last through the night, but she hired me anyhow. I did last the night, but just barely. The job was back-breaking. After business slowed for the evening, Shelia, who doubled as the cook, sat at a table and got hammered most nights. After the first night she apologized for getting drunk, saying that was not very professional. I got a kick out of her. She was a real character. All the employees smoked at the table next to my area. After about three weeks, my lungs hurt. I told her I had to quit. Sheila informed me that I wasn't allowed to quit until she'd found a replacement. I was pretty sure she was wrong about that, but I found a replacement for her that night back at the hostel. End of dishwashing job at Mexican café.

The hostel had a rule that no one could stay for more than three weeks. At the end of three weeks, I secured a bed at another hostel. They didn't have a time limit and my bed had an ocean view. The atmosphere was much looser at this hostel. The place was also filthy, with dirty, stinky dishes always piled in the sink and on the counters. Many nights the managers had loud drunken parties downstairs in the picnic area.

I bought a red bikini and sewed some white fuzzy feathers around the edges of the top and bottom. I showed it to the women in the dorm and they all liked it. I bought a Santa hat and was all ready for Christmas day. I spent Christmas with Steve, Melanie, and another friend from the hostel. I'd bought Melanie and Steve bike water bottles. I told Mel that she would get a bike for Christmas, which turned out to be true. We walked over to my first hostel and wished Miguel a Merry Christmas; then we went to the beach. I wore my Santa bikini and Steve took pictures of me. We stopped at a produce stand and drank from a coconut together. It was the best Christmas ever, just as I'd imagined it. "Somewhere over the Rainbow"—the Hawaiian version.

One morning Mel and I were traveling to the North Shore by bus when an elderly woman climbed on and, after taking a seat, put a harmonica holder around her neck, pulled out a ukulele, and started playing some beautiful music. I looked at Mel and said I felt like I was in a movie, to which she replied, "We are." There were many magical moments like that on the island.

I often walked the beach at Hanalei Bay, on the North Shore, the most spectacular beach I had ever seen. As I walked on the sand, the ocean was on my right and on my left was a breathtaking view of the mountains. I had never seen anything like it. Not far away was the beach where the famous scene in *From Here to Eternity* was filmed. The North Shore was a fabulous jungle and rain forest, surrounded by beaches. Farther north was the Na Pali Coast, with an eleven-mile hike into Kalalau Valley. I'd heard of the coast and the famous hike even before I arrived. I knew in my heart that one day I'd be hiking the coast and bought hiking sandals from the shoe store specifically for that purpose. Somehow I was meant to go there.

After living at the second hostel for a few weeks, money became scarce. I asked the managers of both hostels if there were any positions open for a work trade arrangement, but none was available. The day arrived when I had only enough money to pay for one more night. I decided that I'd eat a good meal and sleep on clean sheets. I didn't know what would come the following day, but that day I was a queen.

The following morning I asked Jeff, one of the tenants, if he'd give me and my luggage a ride. I didn't know where I'd go, but at least I had a ride. I wasn't scared or even concerned. As I sat there eating my breakfast and wondering where I would sleep that night, I noticed that one of the women who was on work trade was packing up her belongings. She was moving out! The manager approached me, asked if she could talk to me, and gave me the position. She told me that the woman hadn't been fired, but chose to leave on her own. I'd have a bed to sleep in for as long as I cleaned my assigned area two hours each day.

I requested cleaning supplies, bleach, gloves, and a mask. The one bathroom, in which at least twenty-five people showered each day, had never been cleaner. I was responsible for two half-baths, one full bathroom, the downstairs party picnic area, and inside dorms. It would be okay short term, but not much more. I'd lived in my own little sparkling-clean Linda world for many, many years;

this was quite the opposite. It was amazing how flexible I could be when the situation called for it, but it got old—fast.

A few weeks later, the woman who'd left that morning, giving me the opportunity to do work trade, came by for a visit. I was very happy to thank her in person. I told her how I had run out of money with no place to go that day. She told me that she hadn't planned to leave, but for some reason decided to go on the spur of the moment. She had a car but had nowhere to go either. Later that day, she found a room in a house with some friends and another job. She said that it all worked out for the best, because she'd become very unhappy working at the hostel. Now she was happy. It was amazing to me how it had all unfolded.

The owner of the hostel was a real "piece of work," as they say. One day he'd seen me riding my bike and asked if he could join me on a ride. I instinctively wanted to say no but didn't want to be rude, so I said yes instead. We rode to the beach together and when we returned, he invited me to go to the drug store to pick up a few things. My Christmas pictures were ready, so I rode along with him. I was looking at the pictures at the store and he saw me in the Santa bikini. He suggested that we go back to the hostel, grab my bikini, and hot-tub at his house. I did nothing to hide my revulsion at the thought of his Santa Claus body and hideous suggestion. My smiling face turned into a grimace as I said, "No way, forget it." I had the distinct feeling that he was no stranger to that reaction. He gave me a ride back to the hostel. The next day I told the manager what had happened. She said Santa Body was gross, and that he made such inappropriate suggestions to guests all the time.

Fortunately, he was so pleased with my cleaning that he let me be. He had a bad temper and was known to fire people on the spot for no good reason, so I was afraid he would kick me out. I was glad he didn't but knew I needed to find another place to live. The fact that he could go on a rampage and I could be out on the street at a moment's notice, coupled with the parties at night, created too much stress in my life. And this was supposed to be paradise!

Mel was working at the coffee shop across the street and I'd sometimes drop by to see her. One morning she asked me how life was at the hostel. I replied, "It's less and less like the Ritz every day." She knew exactly what I meant. We both laughed, and I silently prayed to find a different living situation soon.

The drug store put my pictures on disc, and I emailed them along with holiday greetings and the announcement that I'd moved to Kauai to my family and friends.

I was invited to stay with a couple in the North Shore for a time and when that ran its course I started to let go of even more of my belongings. Once again, I woke up every morning with the tremendous compulsion to get rid of things. I just went with it and became much more mobile. My top priority became finding inner peace. I walked the beach on Hanalei Bay and stood in the center of a big circle that someone had drawn in the sand one afternoon. I faced the sun with my head tilted upward and my eyes closed. I was deep into meditation when I felt and heard something sniffing and snorting. I opened my eyes and a big bulldog was walking around the edge of the circle, sniffing the air, but not entering. I couldn't help but smile when I noticed a Chinese man standing nearby. He smiled too and called his dog away. I closed my eyes and finished meditating. When I finished, I could see the Chinese man standing off to the side, also meditating.

I began to walk away, and he approached me and said, "Are you a teacher?" I said, "Yes, aren't we all?" He smiled and we introduced ourselves. Wei said that he had many things to teach me if I was open to learning them. That day he told me how after years of meditation, his body was moved, exercised, and stretched by some higher force from within. He said that it occurred every day. He told me that if I dropped all of my rituals and practices, there would be nothing I "had" to do and I'd be free.

After our initial meeting on the beach, I ran into him frequently there and we talked, or he called me, or I called him and asked to meet. I called Wei to tell him that I needed to move out of the condo but had no idea where I'd live. He said, "That is very good." He told me it would all work out. The next day, I was drawn to go to a little bakery in Kapaa. My inner voice directed me to go there to meet someone who'd give me a place to stay—and that is exactly what happened. An older woman, who took a few hundred dollars' worth of clothing and household items I was giving away, worked out a trade with me. She had a one-bedroom condo. In exchange for organizing her condo, I would receive lodging for a week-and-a-half. She had a friend who said I could go to her house next.

I worked my butt off on that woman's condo. She worked me like a dog. Within several days her entire place was de-cluttered and completely reorganized. At the end of one week, she came home from work and announced that she couldn't let me sleep on her couch another night, even though her friend was scheduled to pick me up the next day. She told me I had to leave that night, and it was already dark. I told her I had no money and nowhere to go. She was unmoved, but told me she'd meet me at the hostel, where she'd pay for one night.

I hurriedly packed my things and loaded them into her car. I rode my bike the few miles to the hostel, in the cold dark night, and she met me there. She asked if her friend could pick me up the following day. I said, "No, I will not be going to your friend's house." She gave me twenty-five dollars to pay for an overnight stay. To keep from crying and totally losing it, I repeated to myself that everything was okay and it would all work out. I thanked her and walked toward the entrance of the hostel. Heavy rains had soaked my mattress and mosquitoes swarmed me all night, biting my face and any exposed areas. I barely slept.

The next day I found Chris. We put together a little shelter made from tarps, up in the brush and the trees on a nearby hillside, not far from where his campsite was. We took my luggage—I was down to two pieces by then—and hid them in the bushes. I was crying. I told Chris that I just wanted a place of my own to live in and to be happy. He looked at me with understanding eyes and said, "I know." I slept in the outdoor shelter that night on top of a thick layer of pine needles; the sound of the wind whipping the tarp around woke me up off and on all night.

The time had come for me to hike into Na Pali Coast.

CHAPTER NINETEEN

I relentlessly persisted in trying to create my life for more than twenty years. At times my situation temporarily improved, but I always found myself back at square one. My addictions to cigarettes, alcohol, and drugs fell away as I awakened to each higher truth—none too soon, as I might not be here if I'd continued to use. In retrospect I can see that I was progressing far more than I realized at the time. All of the teachings I studied were steps in the ladder of my spiritual awakening. I am deeply grateful to every one of my teachers, because each one literally helped keep me alive in this world of form throughout the most difficult years of my life.

Still, my major life lessons and core issues—lack of safety and security, along with immense guilt—were incessantly running my life. I relived the insanity of the same day over and over. Through nearly fifty moves covering ten states and twenty-some cities, the names, faces, and jobs changed, but the same problems and patterns kept repeating. My hike in Hawaii had been the adventure of a lifetime, both spiritually and physically, resulting in a true awakening of my will to live. Yet life didn't immediately run smoothly in the aftermath.

I found a job in a café in Kauai and rented a room in a charming little house nearby. Before I knew it, I had fallen back into the regular daily grind. With the high cost of rent and food I did little more than survive and had no energy left over to even think about writing. I'd never worked so hard for so little. I decided that it was just too difficult and expensive to stay in Hawaii—it was time to go back to California. Kauai was an incredible adventure, one I would always have with me. It had changed me in many vital, indefinable ways.

I had done so much inner work in my life. And it was true that my life was improving. It was still falling apart outwardly, but improving from within. Back in California I worked some more crappy jobs and moved around a few more times. I soon realized I could no longer work at unfulfilling, meaningless jobs, because something inside wouldn't let me. There was something I was born to do and had to do *now*—write. This almost insane desire caused me to wind up in desperate straits once again—broke and homeless—but determined.

Then, through a miraculous series of events, I was guided to find a literary agent, an apartment, some part-time work, and even a computer to write on. I wrote for a month, but the book wasn't flowing the way I wanted it to. Over tea at a local coffee shop, Dave, the manager of the bookstore at Seaside Center for Spiritual Living and who had recently ordered ten copies of my self-published book, recommended I read a book that was very popular there. It was titled *The Disappearance of the Universe* by Gary R. Renard—and being guided to this book was a huge, gigantic, life-changing moment for me.

The Disappearance of the Universe explains that we are not creating our reality here, moment by moment. It was all created at a higher level. This is all a script that we are merely following, and God has nothing to do with this world. Take heart, God has not abandoned us—*au contraire*, my dear friends. We are in Heaven with God right now because we never left. None of this is real, we are only imagining that we are separate from God, and everything in this world is a projection of that imagined separation. This is all a dream and is no more real than the dreams we have while sleeping, from which we will eventually awaken and see that we are really and truly with God. The *appearance* of being separate from one another and God—which is what the ego is—is false.

Reading all this and trying to grasp its principles upset me a great deal initially, because many of the spiritual teachings that I'd been studying for the past twenty years promised that I could create my day-to-day reality. They claimed that this reality can be Heaven, and God created all of it. After reading *The Disappearance of the Universe,* I was thrown for a loop. I felt depressed and discouraged, but then realized that Mr. Renard taught a radically different kind of forgiveness that undoes the ego, which will eventually lead us back to our real home. It all began to make sense. I became enthralled with his teachings.

Specific forgiveness techniques were outlined in Mr. Renard's books, and I used them as instructed. But it was more than the techniques themselves; it was how I applied them, along with the deep understanding of the true forgiveness principles, that made the difference in my life. I felt more confident and peaceful. I felt like I was making quantum leaps in my forgiveness and spiritual awakening. This was a feeling I'd never before experienced. I shared the information with friends, and they also began reaping positive results using the techniques.

I realized at some point during this time of awakening that it was *me* I needed to forgive more than anyone else regarding my past. I came to understand that life is eternal; that I am immortal spirit, not this body; and that I cannot be damaged. This realization allowed me to end my suffering once and for all, as I was no longer defined by my body or what had happened to it.

Within a few weeks, people responded more positively toward me. From the same book I began using a form of prayer during meditation. I felt inspired with new ideas and acted upon them. One thing led to another. After reading Mr. Renard's second book, *Your Immortal Reality*, I applied the accelerated true forgiveness techniques from that book to my life, which worked incredibly well. I bought his Enlightenment Cards and read a few of them each day. I felt my inner life transforming, and my outer relationships began to change as well. Many of us know just how challenging some of the relationships with parents and siblings can be, and it was no different in my case. Through the practice of forgiveness, my relationship within myself became more whole, resulting in a more whole relationship with my mom and sister, not to mention all of my "outer" relationships. It was and continues to be incredible to witness. We are now closer, as a family, than I ever dreamed possible. It was as though I'd died a million times, to finally be able to live this one time. Where I once saw an endless maze of walls and obstacles, I saw a flowing landscape of opportunity. Like Mr. Renard's teachings, my other teachers also spoke of working at the level of cause—the mind—rather than at the level of effect—the physical world. After all those years I had a good understanding of that truth. Now, with true forgiveness, I had a tool that was very effective in working at the level of cause.

I was so inspired that I soon felt guided to teach a workshop on The Wisdom of True Forgiveness and placed an outline on my website. I emailed Mr. Renard to ask permission to use his teachings, and also to invite him to lunch when he was in San Diego to lead an upcoming workshop. When I sent the email, I felt a wave come over me. I knew we'd meet. The next day, I was reading his reply granting his permission and accepting my invitation. As we continued to correspond, I told him that I was writing my life story and was using his true forgiveness teachings to heal the traumas of my childhood, and that I'd scheduled my first workshop at the same local coffee shop where I was first introduced to his book.

After reading *The Disappearance of the Universe,* my original idea
for writing a book was replaced with the inspiration to write this
story, although I had never previously imagined it was possible. It
was like the book wrote me, rather than the other way around. It
was an otherworldly experience.

A couple of weeks later, my friend Diane and I picked up Gary
Renard at his hotel and brought him to Cristina's Lemon Grove
restaurant for lunch. On the way to the restaurant Gary and I
began talking about how I forgave the traumas and tragedies of my
life using his techniques. As we climbed out of the car and made
our way into the restaurant, I told Gary how grateful I was for his
teachings and he gave me a warm hug. During lunch I asked him
if he'd be willing to read my manuscript and perhaps give me permission to use his teachings in my book. Gary told me that I could
use anything of his I wanted and he promised to read my manuscript.

Lunch was delicious; Gary, a meat and potatoes man, seemed
to enjoy his first raw gourmet meal. Cristina graciously treated us
all. Then we headed north to my favorite Moonlight Beach for a
walk. Gary seemed to love the beach as much as Diane and I. I
took his hands in mine and looked into his eyes as I thanked him
for opening my mind to the truths that changed everything. I
drove him back to his hotel and we hugged our good-byes. It was
the start of one of the most valuable friendships I've ever had and
continue to be privileged to enjoy to this day.

With his powerful knowledge I was able to undo the insanity
that was my life! True forgiveness gives me a way to make quantum leaps toward a different day. It had been quite a climb, but
every step was necessary to deliver me to this point. All my life I
thought that if only I had more money, the perfect relationship, the
perfect job, and the perfect place to live that I'd be all right. But

what I was really after was how I thought I'd feel if I had all of those things, which is inner peace, which is real and lasting and the only thing that is of any value. We can't see it, touch it, smell it, hear it, or taste it, but once we awaken to it, we'll never lose it or be without it again. It is not a temporary experience we have; it is what we truly are.

World peace is an inside job, one mind at a time. Ultimately, that is what this book is about. Until we have peace within our own minds and homes, we will not have peace within our world. Through the use of the techniques of true forgiveness in my everyday life, I increasingly feel more of who I am as I undo the false layers of the ego mind. I am now awakened to the truth that since none of this is real and I am really with God right now, there is nothing to feel guilty about. We are ALL totally innocent. True forgiveness has returned me to my innocence. Now I wake up each day and see the world with the wide-eyed purity of a child, just happy to be alive. I'm still dancing on bars and tables to "Brick House," but now I'm doing it free of the addictions that once weighed me down. I like to call this feeling Peace of my Heart. This is a part of what forgiveness gives to me.

I now realize that all the varying degrees of crime, violence, poverty, death, disease, all our differences such as sexual preference, skin color, physical features, culture, language, religion, political allegiances, all prejudice, and the guilt and punishment that follow all the alleged "wrongs" are all simply symbols of our imagined separation from God. They are nothing more than a mirror showing us to ourselves. In Heaven there is no male or female nor any other differences—there is only the one. But we've forgotten our true reality and have become so used to the world as it is that we have accepted it as our true reality. We spend much of our time trying to make this world into Heaven. As we can all clearly see, it is not working because Hell, or separation from God, will never be

Heaven. As we each awaken to the truth that we are all one and the same, these symbols of separation will fade from view. Love is love, and is always the answer, no matter the issue. When we change our perception of the world from within, we will end our suffering. After that, what does or doesn't occur "out there" will no longer matter and no longer be our focus.

Somewhere along the way I became conscious that as long as someone somewhere in the world is being blown up, raped, beaten, or dying of starvation or disease, I know I am not in Heaven because none of that exists or could exist in the real Heaven. Real Heaven is a place where every block is filled with nothing but Heaven. It is impossible for God to be perfect love and be a part of the insanity of this world. The illusion of Heaven here on Earth is merely a way for the ego to distract us from seeking to know the truth of our existence. It is all a trick, which will eventually fall apart, and is nothing in comparison to the real Heaven. After a while, I became relieved to know that it is ego and not God that is creating the illusion of this world. Knowing that my true Home is in Heaven with God and that every time I truly forgive, I am one step closer to my true Home is what makes me feel safe and provided for, like nothing in this world ever has or ever will. Knowing that God is my one and only true source gives my life meaning and purpose beyond anything I have ever known or could have dreamed. Knowing that in ultimate reality, I am sinless, undamaged, perfect, and never alone is what makes me fearless in the midst of this world of shattered dreams and seemingly real nightmares. Heaven is perfect oneness with God and is the state to which we will someday return, permanently.

Once I understood that I have about as much control over this world as a gnat has over a sandstorm, I was able to stop spinning my wheels. While our script is already written and we are merely experiencing it, it is possible to switch to different outcomes. That is another aspect of what forgiveness gives to me. I'm no longer living the same day over and over. I'm careful to not become dependent on anything outside of me for my happiness. I accept that this world is one hell of a crazy place. However, I've found that "out there" has become a much more pleasant experience as I awaken and continually switch outcomes. As long as I remember to choose the Holy Spirit mind, instead of the ego mind, the only two actual choices we have in this world, I am able to maintain my balance and live in peace no matter what appears to be happening. Regardless of whether or not we have the partner, money, career, house, car, or perfect butt and thighs, there is no escaping these truths. Believe me, I've tried every way known to woman.

My best friend one day can be my enemy the next, and my enemy can turn into a new best friend. A person will love you up one side and down the other one day, and then rub salt in your wounds the next. Someone might hit you over the head and slap you in the face with your own neuroses, leaving you gasping for air. They can make you queen or king, give you a castle to live in and buckets of money, or toss you out on the street begging for food. One day they will give you accolades for your brilliance, and the next pee in your oatmeal. And "they" are us, every one of "them." We are one mind appearing as many bodies, and all of it is just a projection of our one mind. I do my best to avoid becoming too attached to the perceived good and the supposed bad. I take none of it seriously, do what I love, laugh often, and forgive it all.

So far in this experience of life, what has been most rewarding and fulfilling to me is to share this message with others. There is nothing else that brings more joy and light into my life than to bring joy and light to another. It is what makes this journey viable and worthwhile. As I forgive my way Home to God, I feel honored, privileged, and deeply grateful that just maybe I have something of value to share with another. I was born on the twelfth anniversary of the dropping of the bomb on Hiroshima, and as much as that event was a catalyst of horrendous devastation that ripped our world apart, I know in my heart that the power of the message I have to share is a far more powerful catalyst, capable of bringing our world back together in ways beyond our wildest imaginings. I'm not claiming to be a great writer or speaker, because I know that it is the message of true forgiveness that is truly great. I'm merely a student like everyone else, with much to learn and a long way to go.

The telling of this story revealed to me how rich I am through all my friends and family who have supported, encouraged, and loved me, never more powerfully than now. I came here to California to build my life from the inside out. I've accomplished that and more. I am the kingdom that my forgiveness and peace have built. As I sit here in my little apartment near the beach, I know that the writing of this book and the forgiveness of my life have made me rich and full beyond anything I ever could have dreamed. Wherever I am is a palace, and everyone I meet is God. I can see a vision in my mind's eye of light pouring down from above, cascading sparkling light on a naked baby dancing on the air. Her arms are raised high and she laughs with delight as she grows into the girl who becomes the powerful woman, realizing that all she has endured happened in the time it takes a snowflake to pass by and melt. Just as quickly she awakens from the dream and is once again within the arms of God and in the peace of Heaven.

Like most of us, all I ever wanted since I was a little girl was to simply be happy. I didn't care about big houses, fancy cars, clothes, jewelry, or a "career." What I cared about was family. At the age of fifty-one I think that I've finally found my way to living happily, and everywhere I go I feel like I am with "family," because of the love that fills my heart. All that I thought I'd lost is inconsequential in light of what I've gained. In true reality I've given up nothing of value in order to have everything. I am no longer broken. That is all that matters. *I . . . am . . . no . . . longer . . . broken . . .* That is my greatest success and one I couldn't have imagined in my wildest dreams. I cannot express in words how that feels: to not be broken. It is simply something that must be felt and experienced, and if it is possible for me, it is possible for others too.

Out of the corner of my right eye, as I am nearing the end of this story, I see a light about two feet off the ground. It is a very bright white, with a few shades of pink and green showing faintly around the edges. The light flashes out from a mid-point and then spreads out horizontally. This all happens in less than an instant. As soon as I turn my head to get a better look, it is gone. This is not a mind vision—I see that flash the same way I see my fingers on the keyboard. After about twenty-four hours of processing, I realize what was communicated to me in a flash of feeling and thought. I was given a peek of Heaven.

When I began writing this story, I asked Jesus to please give me a glimpse of Heaven and he said that he would at the end of this story. I'd forgotten that conversation until now. Now I realize that the light I saw was a small glimpse of Heaven, and it was not covering this world up or hiding it. This world did not disappear. I could actually see that this world doesn't really exist, and that Heaven is all there is. More than seeing Heaven, I felt Heaven and God with all that I am. I felt pure truth. I said, "Thank you, Jesus, for being a man who keeps his word, and who gives me something about HOME to write about." Jesus said, *"And this is just the beginning."*

Now that I know that none of this really happened and this is all just a dream, I could have saved myself more than a thousand hours of writing spread over three-hundred-seventy-one days and nights, and the fifty years—perhaps lifetimes—of dreaming to produce a story that could have been written in just two words. It is actually the only true story that exists and would ever need be written.

GOD IS

I imagine Jesus and me rocking out to a very special performance of . . . The Staple Singers singing, "I know a place ain't nobody cryin', ain't nobody worried. No more smilin' faces lyin' to the races. I'll take you there . . ."

—The Beginning—

Appendix I

Summary of True Forgiveness
Techniques and Teachings

INTRODUCTION

The following teachings and techniques are adapted from the books by Gary R. Renard.

Mr. Renard's books teach the metaphysics of *A Course In Miracles,* which in my case enabled me to have a better understanding of the course and as a result, along with many countless others, facilitated my becoming a student of the course. It has been said that if the course is the can, Mr. Renard's books are a can opener. One of the goals of *A Course In Miracles* is to teach us to replace automatic judgment with automatic forgiveness. The course assists us in undoing the ego mind through a series of mind training exercises. The true forgiveness referred to here and in my story is different from the old-fashioned forgiveness where we say, "I forgive you even though you are wrong." True forgiveness recognizes that we are all suffering from the same disease, which is our imagined separation from God, and therefore we are all equally innocent. This is the same kind of forgiveness that Jesus taught and practiced during his last lifetime on Earth. It is the same kind of forgiveness that is taught in *A Course In Miracles,* of which Jesus is the voice. The healing that occurs through true forgiveness is powerful beyond imagination. The following summary is only intended as an introduction to the teachings of true forgiveness. If you are truly interested in learning more, I highly recommend that you read Mr. Renard's books and *A Course In Miracles*. It is a full and deep understanding of the teachings behind the forgiveness techniques that makes them so powerful. By utilizing these teachings and techniques I was able to stop my own suffering, switch outcomes, and live a new day. Finally!

SUMMARY OF TEACHINGS

A Course In Miracles teaches that there are two worlds: the world of God and the world of man. Only one is real: the world of God. There never was, nor will there ever be, a time when we are not in Heaven. We had a tiny, mad idea and imagined we could be separate from God. The thought of separation is ego. The ego is not real and is nothing more than a false thought. The ego mind created the illusion of this world. True forgiveness undoes the ego mind, which will dispel this dream and awaken us to our true world, which is Heaven with God.

When we imagined our separation from God, we felt guilty. Punishment followed the guilt. Our ego mind projected the guilt outward. Our bodies and everything in this world are merely projections of our ego mind. No one is guilty because none of this is real. We are all innocent. Because all others are a projection of our ego mind, when we forgive another we really forgive ourselves. Think of this, and forgive all those whom you would judge. Replace judgment, arguing, and complaining with true forgiveness. Judgment, arguing, and complaining keep us stuck in our ego mind. True forgiveness keeps us in Holy Spirit mind, undoes the ego, ends our suffering, and awakens us. Eventually, there will be nothing between us and our total awareness of perfect oneness with God. Because God's mind is totally pure, so must ours be in order to rejoin with God.

We have two choices, every second of every day, ego mind or Holy Spirit mind. The ego mind keeps us stuck, and the Holy Spirit mind sets us free. With the ego mind, we live the insanity of the same day, over and over. With the Holy Spirit mind, we switch to different outcomes, enabling us to live a different day, as we make our way home. Jesus/Holy Spirit/Higher Self are always available to guide us. Ask for guidance and it will be given. None of this is real; it is only a projection of our mind. When we forgive, the Holy Spirit mind takes care of the rest. We are one mind appearing as many bodies.

Suggested Five-Minute Meditations for Morning and Evening

In meditation, visualize taking Jesus' hand and going to God. Think of laying everything we think we need to be happy in this world on the altar before God. They become our gifts to God. Tell God that he is our one and only source. Tell God how much you love him and how grateful you are to be completely taken care of by him, forever safe and secure. Then become silent. Have the attitude that you are as God created you, not a body but just like him, and that you will be with him forever. Then let go of everything, joining with God's love, and become lost in joyful communion with him.

Later, as we go about our daily life, inspired ideas will usually come to us that are in answer to our prayers. Suggested reading also includes some of Gary Renard's Enlightenment Cards each day for further acceleration of progress toward spiritual enlightenment.

The thoughts expressed on the cards were spoken by Gary's Ascended Master Teachers and were chosen with their guidance.

Techniques to Accelerate True Forgiveness

Use these through all waking hours as needed.

To forgive your self or stop blaming yourself. Say to your self and/or say while looking into a mirror: I am immortal spirit. This body is just an image that has nothing to do with what I am.

To forgive another. Say mind to mind to another: You are spirit, whole and innocent. All is forgiven and released.

Throughout the day, as we feel the need to forgive, the preceding techniques can be used. Ask the Holy Spirit to guide you through this process of forgiveness, for the big things as well as the little things that happen each day. Big matters or small, they are equally illusory. This can be done anywhere, mind to mind or in meditation. If done in meditation, visualize an image of whom you are forgiving, say the forgiveness technique slowly three times, and allow the image to disappear from your view. The one you want to forgive the least is the one you need to forgive the most, for your own sake.

Appendix II

Another Note from the Author

While I was writing the section of the book where it is revealed that my sister Cathy was raped, I was shown on a spiritual level the worldwide scope of the problem of unreported sexual assaults and abuse. Cathy and I are far from alone. Read on.

There were rumors of at least two other unreported gang-rapes of girls I knew from school. I know of at least four other women who were raped and never reported it. When I ask students at my workshops who among them have suffered from unreported sexual assault or abuse, or know of someone who has, the majority of people, men and women alike, raise their hands. How many other families are there out there like ours? How many of the women and men I've met and known have been raped, but never reported it? How many others are suffering in silence? This is not just a woman's issue. Rape, molestation, and all sexual assaults cross all barriers and its victims are all ages and genders.

The number of unreported rapes must be staggering. And there must be an equally staggering number of unreported and unidentified rapists and molesters living among us, free to rape again. These perpetrators are dependent upon the victims being paralyzed into silence by fear, guilt, and shame. It seems chillingly apparent that many of these perpetrators are our relatives or people who hold positions of trust within our communities, those who easily slip into our lives and blend, undetected. This cycle of abuse is a menacing and crippling legacy that has been passed down from one generation to the next. If we knew the true number, we'd be shaken to our core. It is a silent and invisible epidemic of massive proportions, the devastating effects of which are beyond measure. Its silence and invisibility allow the disease to flood our planet and we are drowning in its ooze. It is time to break the silence and to tell the truth. In the light of the truth, the darkness of the epidemic will disappear and healing will take place.

The reason that things appear so out of control is because we have given up, mistakenly thinking that we are powerless. The opposite is true. We have the power within our own minds to eradicate this monstrous epidemic. In fact, it is only within our minds that we can eradicate this epidemic, because that is where the damage lingers and exists. True forgiveness is a way to release the damage of past abuses and assaults. Our power is in knowing that we are immortal spirit, not our bodies, and that this is a spiritual problem, not a physical one.

It is impossible to be both a body and an immortal spirit. Our current experiences are a direct result of what we are choosing at any given moment. When we choose to make our bodies real, we become stuck in the everyday suffering of providing for the body—an endless pit of need. At the same time we feel the guilt of what our bodies and other bodies are doing that appears to be wrong and damaging. When we choose to experience ourselves as immortal spirits, we have the advantage of no longer being defined and ruled by what the body thinks it needs, or by its past.

The realization that we are not these bodies is a truth that will set us free . . . from our suffering.

Our true power and freedom will come from using the truth to undo the insanity of this world. The war out there is really a war from within, and so the revolution must be fought and won from within also. I see the light of truth, shining all over the world, obliterating all darkness in its path, like a blanket of new clover over a forest floor that had once been desecrated by fire. If I can heal from my molestations, abuse, and rape, through true forgiveness, then so can others. Through healing and making the epidemic visible, we can stop this cycle of abuse and violent assault.

As I forgave, I awakened to the truth that I came into this world with major issues of safety, security, shame, and guilt, which on a higher level caused this life to unfold as it did. I could see that the world was not being done to me. The world was being done *by* me. All the people and events in my life were symbolic of my imagined separation from God. All the people and events of my life were showing me the contents of my unconscious, reminding me of how I felt at the original imagined separation from God. And while the rape of my body and deaths of my loved ones were especially difficult and the most painful events of my life, I could see that the same feelings of shame, fear, loneliness, and guilt were consistently felt throughout my life in varying degrees, through my many different life events, resulting in the suicidal depression from which I suffered for most of my life prior to this awakening.

I feel that the pain of the separation from God and the guilt that followed were purposely intense for me during this lifetime in order to facilitate my awakening. It only appeared that the psychic wounds of my childhood traumas caused me to think and behave in insane and self-destructive ways. The truth is that I was born wounded and my script was already set. The pain of separation is felt every day and in many ways by each of us, and no one is required to go through what I went through in order to facilitate their own awakening. This just happened to be my path. The message of true forgiveness brings with it an end to suffering from trauma and tragedy, so I am deeply grateful that I am able to facilitate my awakening the way I am and I see all that has happened to me as true blessings in my life. There is nothing I'd change, even if I could. There is no need to, because I see it all as a dream that no longer defines me. *It is through the forgiveness of life's greatest tragedies that we are given the gift of our greatest opportunities to heal and awaken to what we truly are. Our attackers and abusers can be counted among our greatest spiritual teachers, if we choose forgiveness.*

I have found that those I wish to forgive the least are the ones I need to forgive the most, for my own sake. It is important to know how we see another is ultimately how we see ourselves. To see another as guilty is to see myself as guilty. To see another as spirit, whole and innocent, is to see myself as whole and innocent. With forgiveness comes inner peace along the way to making our way Home. The magnificence of perfect oneness with God is the only thing that will ever truly satisfy us. When you've had enough of this illusion you'll move mountains to get back to it.

As long as we appear to be in these bodies, there are things we will appear to do here in this illusion. Until one becomes proficient in forgiveness, there is no need to give up the earthly desires. It will all happen quite naturally and effortlessly. With ego, there is suffering; with Holy Spirit, there is peace. It is always a moment-to-moment choice. It is as simple as that, but not always so easy. Our efforts are more wisely and efficiently spent working from the level of cause, the mind, if your goal is God.

True forgiveness is not about condoning the damaging behavior of others, it is seeing that there is no other than innocent immortal spirit, and it is done for your own sake. Because when you release your brother, you release yourself.

In conclusion, please be advised that true forgiveness is for everyone, everywhere whose peace is the least bit disturbed by what appear to be outer conflicts. Make no mistake that all conflicts, big or small, are equally illusory and are always an opportunity to undo the ego mind, which eventually leads you Home.

All conflict in this world that is not of peace is a symbol of the imagined separation from God and the guilt that follows. We can make true forgiveness our purpose in life, but we must choose it to make it so. This is a story of becoming whole and One Again through the power of TRUE FORGIVENESS. It is free to all, everywhere. I hope you'll join me in spreading these teachings around the world.

—Linda

— ACKNOWLEDGMENTS —

I wish to thank the following people for all their support, encouragement, and love, which have been and will remain beyond measure. It is my intention to thank each and every one of them by sharing the message of True Forgiveness throughout the world.

My literary agent Bill Gladstone and his assistant Ming Russell. My publishers: Bob Friedman, Jack Jennings, Tania Seymour, and everyone else at Hampton Roads Publishing, and my editor Julie McCarron.

My friends and family, Bethanne Abbass, Ginger Adler, Debbie Barilla, Amie Bell, Diane Campbell, Margo Carrera, Jan Cook, Mary Dennis, Tom Donahue, Doris Edmiston, Tracy Firmino, Caleb Furgatch, Cristina, Guillermo, and Regina Guzman, Carol Harvey, Maggie Hodge, Jody Karkowski, David Kennedy, Azim Khamisa, Bill Kiehl, Mike Lasater, Edward Leader, Sharon Lund, Ross and Carole Mariol, Christopher McNeece, Constance Meyerson, Janae Nute, Johan Oeyen, Diane and John Olive, Gary Porter, Karen Renard, Samuel Riche, Chris Riordan, Mike Rocker, Warren Rokos, Jean St. Martin, Nouk Sanchez, Susan Schenk, James Sinclair, Christian Souza, Alex Uma, Gwen Wagner, Mark Waters, Natalie White, Brad Woodard, and last but not least, my nieces and nephew, Kristy, Sarah, and Mike.

I also wish to thank Gary Renard, without whose teachings I'd still be lost; Thomas F. Donahue, for his legal expertise; and my sister Cathy and my mom, who never gave up on me. Finally, thank you to my niece, Sarah Montesi, for the beautiful poems at the beginning of parts 1, 2, and 3; and Karen Renard, my sister Cathy, Phil Latzy, and Michael Perlin (www.starseedfilms.com), for their inspirations and contributions to the book's cover.

— RESOURCE GUIDE —

The Disappearance of the Universe, by Gary R. Renard
Your Immortal Reality, by Gary R. Renard
Love Has Forgotten No One:
The Answer to Life, by Gary R. Renard
Enlightenment Cards, by Gary R. Renard
www.garyrenard.com

Spoken Miracles: A Companion to the
Disappearance of the Universe, by Abby Lucia Espinosa
Hay House, Inc.
P.O. Box 5100
Carlsbad, CA 92018
760-431-7695 or 800-654-5126
www.hayhouse.com

A Course In Miracles
Foundation for Inner Peace
P.O. Box 598
Mill Valley, CA 94942
415-388-2060
www.acim.org

Take Me to Truth: Undoing the Ego,
by Nouk Sanchez and Tomas Vieira
USA and Canada, NBN, custserv@nbnbooks.com
800-462-6420
www.takemetotruth.com

Closing the Circle, Pursah's Gospel of Thomas,
and A Course in Miracles
by Rogier Fentener van Vlissingen
www.acimnthomas.com
USA and Canada, NBN, custserv@nbnbooks.com
800-462-6420

The Basic State
The Solution in All Problems
www.greatfreedom.org

Radical Honesty, by Dr. Brad Blanton
646 Shuler Lane
Stanley, VA 22851
540-778-2982
www.radicalhonesty.com

Azim's Bardo: From Murder to Forgiveness, by Azim Khamisa
Azim's Bardo: From Forgiveness to Fulfillment, by Azim Khamisa
ANK Publishing, Inc.
8189 Via Mallorca
La Jolla, CA 92037
858-452-2541
www.AzimKhamisa.com

Sacred Living, Sacred Dying: A Guide
to Embracing Life and Death, by Sharon Lund
www.sharonlund.com

OTHER HIGHLY RECOMMENDED
SPIRITUAL TEACHERS

Please refer to your local bookstores, libraries, and the Internet for a wide range of books and teaching materials offered by the following spiritual teachers.

Maya Angelou
Richard Bach
Deepak Chopra
Dr. Wayne Dyer
Louise Hay
Shirley MacLaine
Dan Millman
Don Miguel Ruiz
Eckhart Tolle
Neale Donald Walsch
Marianne Williamson
Gary Zukav

ABOUT THE AUTHOR

L inda Jean McNabb spent nearly twenty years in the corporate business world, first as a claims adjuster and then as a sales representative for several large companies offering various products and services. Linda, who came out of her mother's womb folding her own diapers, then formed and operated her own organizing business. For the past several years, she has moved, organized, and simplified many people's lives in North Carolina and more recently in Southern California, where she currently lives. After living in California and being drawn to a healthier lifestyle, she received training as a raw-food chef. Through that network, she became employed by a world-renowned hospital in Rosarito, Mexico, where she taught several nutrition and food preparation classes each week. Currently, Linda is a personal assistant for Gary R. Renard and conducts workshops on the Wisdom of True Forgiveness (www.lindamcnabb.com).